Brit

GW00338399

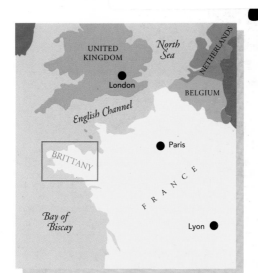

PATRICK DELAFORCE

HarperCollins*Publishers*

YOUR COLLINS TRAVELLER

Your Collins Traveller Guide will help you find your way around your chosen destination quickly and easily. It is colour-coded for easy reference:

The blue section answers the question 'I would like to see or do something; where do I go and what do I see when I get there?' This section is arranged as an alphabetical list of topics and it is recommended that an up-to-date atlas or street plan is used in conjunction with their location maps. Within each topic you will find:
- A selection of the best examples on offer.
- How to get there, costs and opening hours for each entry.
- The outstanding features of each entry.
- A simplified map, with each entry plotted and the nearest landmark or transport access.

The red section is a lively and informative gazetteer. It offers:
- Essential facts about the main places and cultural items.
  What is La Bastille? Who was Michelangelo? Where is Delphi?

The gold section is full of practical and invaluable travel information. It offers:
- Everything you need to know to help you enjoy yourself and get the most out of your time away, from Accommodation through Baby-sitters, Car Hire, Food, Health, Money, Newspapers, Taxis, Telephones to Youth Hostels.

Cross-references:

Type in small capitals – CHURCHES – tells you that more information on an item is available within the topic on churches.

A-Z after an item tells you that more information is available within the gazetteer. Simply look under the appropriate name.

A name in bold – **Holy Cathedral** – also tells you that more information on an item is available in the gazetteer – again simply look up the name.

Paimpont

CONTENTS

■ **CULTURAL/HISTORICAL GAZETTEER**

CONTENTS

■ PRACTICAL INFORMATION GAZETTEER

INTRODUCTION

Brittany, the great peninsula in the northwest corner of France, is popular with both British and Parisian families seeking unspoilt beaches, rolling countryside and outdoor activities. It is composed of four departments. Ille-et-Villaine, with Rennes as its *préfecture* town, is in the east, and immediately to the northwest is the former Côtes du Nord (now Côtes d'Armor), the *préfecture* town of which is St. Brieuc. To the far west is Finistère, with coastline on three sides, and Quimper its *préfecture* town, while Morbihan is in the southwest (*préfecture* town Vannes).

This remote peninsula – 'Finis-terre' means the end of the world – is aptly named, being situated away from the traditional warfaring plains of Picardy, Normandy and Champagne. Indeed, it has been a place of refuge for many years, for Brittany was occupied in the 5th and 6thC by Celts from Britain fleeing the invading Saxons and Angles. Across the English Channel came Welshmen, Westcountrymen, even some Scots and Irish, whose Christian priests evangelized 'Little Britain' and Cornouaille. Beautiful, often formidable, cathedrals are testimony to that early faith.

William Shakespeare mentioned Brittany and the Bretons several times in his plays but was rarely complimentary for, truth to tell, few Bretons have achieved fame. Those who have include Bertrand Du Guesclin, eventually Constable of France, who harassed the English armies at the beginning of the Hundred Years' War; Jacques Cartier, who sailed towards Canada in 1537 and discovered the St. Lawrence River; and Chateaubriand, who wrote romantic verses and literature. However, Bretons were renowned as capable and sometimes infamous seamen. The corsairs were legendary, especially Duguay-Trouin and Surcouf in the 18thC, and many of the northern ports owed their prosperity to booty gained by piracy.

Leaving the towns and coastline behind, minor roads will lead you to some of the curiosities for which the region is best known. The strange megalithic site of Carnac has nearly 4000 upright stones in martial lines, laboriously hauled many miles and erected by a race of seafarers four or five thousand years BC. The beautiful collection of 20 villages inland from Brest is home to the 17thC parish closes (*enclos paroissiaux*), unique in Europe, while the great religious processions known as

Palais du Parlement, Rennes

pardons take place between Easter and Christmas all over western Brittany.

Brittany is a curious mixture of the eminently practical and the romantic and spiritual. Tourism is a major money-spinner, albeit concentrated into three months of the year, with efficient tourist offices in the main towns. But fishing is also very important to the region; Concarneau, Cancale, Lorient and a dozen other ports provide fish and shellfish for a wide area. And in the hinterland vast quantities of fruit,

including apples for cider, and vegetables are grown. In contrast to this business-like approach, Brittany keeps alive the legends of King Arthur (Paimpont Forest), Tristan and Isolde of Cornouaille and King Gradlon of Is (Douarnenez). The holy fountains, places of pilgrimage and the special saints (Ste Anne, the Virgin's mother, and St. Yves, the 13thC advocate of justice) all have a permanent place in western Brittany. Nowhere is this independence of spirit more noticeable than in the Breton language, still thriving with over 60 societies and many folklore events throughout the region. Breton costume, with lacy headdresses (*coiffes*) for the ladies, can still be seen at pardons and *fest-noz* (folk celebrations), while many folklore museums help maintain the old traditions. Although not in the culinary league of Burgundy or Provence, *la bonne table* in Brittany always looks inviting. Nearly every restaurant will have one or more delicious fish dishes – *moules marinières*, oysters, lobsters, langoustines and, from the rivers, salmon and trout. You will also find creperies everywhere offering their delicate square pancakes filled with either sweet or savoury fillings, and in every Breton town and most villages you can eat well for under 100F, including a bottle of cider. There are no local wines, but Muscadet and Gros-Plant white and rosé are grown just north of Nantes and are widely available to complement the Breton cuisine.

Quimper

Most British people with families naturally visit Brittany in the school holidays, as indeed do French families, though there are plenty of camp sites and hotels to accommodate this influx, which often triples the local population. However, the best time to visit is out of season, in spring, early summer or the autumn, when the spectacular sights of St. Malo, Concarneau's Ville Close, Locronan, Pont-Aven and Dinan can be seen with a degree of comfort. You should expect a mild climate, laced with a salty breeze and gales in winter. It is wise to take rainwear whenever you go, as a precaution.

For active visitors there are 30 marinas along the coast, a score of off-shore islands and two large nature parks (Armorique and Brière) to explore, rivers and canals on which to rent boats or canoes, windsurfing, sand yachting and underwater exploration. There are also 4000 km of Grandes Randonnées waymarked walks, over 3000 km of bridle paths, 30 riding centres and 150 cycling clubs, as well as tennis courts in most towns and villages.

For the less active there are bird-watching sanctuaries, open-air zoos and lighthouses to visit, fishing in 37 canalized rivers, horse-drawn calèches and the lure of the many golf courses.

But if it's relaxation you're after you could stay at one of the eleven marine hydrotherapy institutes where sea-water treatment tones up the body. And when it rains there are always 60 or more museums and 50 chateaux, including Josselin, Fougères and Vitré, to choose from. And while you're travelling from one attraction to the next, you can keep a look out for roadside calvaries, menhirs amid the bracken, cliff-top chapels, live-lobster farms, seaweed collectors, fishing boats off the point and unusual village artisans. With its fine sandy beaches, colourful cuisine and friendly people, Brittany is the ideal place for a relaxed, good-value holiday – and it's all just a ferry-crossing away!

Rennes

Penfeld

Bd. J. Moulin

Rue d'Algésiras

Av. Georges Clemenceau

Pl. de la Liberté

Rue Jean

Rue Colbert

ÉGLISE ST. LOUIS

Rue de Lyon

CONSERVATOIRE BOTANIQUE NATIONAL DU STANGALAR

LE MÉMORIAL FORT MONTBAREY, TOUR TANGUY & MUSÉE DE VIEUX BREST

Rue J. Macé

Rue Siam

Rue de d'Aiguillon

Pl. Wilson

Pont de Recouvrance

MUSÉE DES BEAUX-ARTS

Rue du Château

Rue Voltaire

Rue P. Brossalette

Bd. de la Marine

Rue Denver

Cours Dajot

Av. S. Penguer

CHÂTEAU DE BREST

Av. F. Roosevelt

Rue J. M. Le Bris

OCEANOPOLIS

Port de Commerce

Attractions

CHÂTEAU DE BREST Southwest corner of the town, near SNCF.
■ 0900-1200, 1400-1800 Wed.-Mon. ● 27F.
Once a 3rdC Roman camp, but rebuilt by Vauban, Colbert and Richelieu, it now houses the mairie, préfecture and Musée de la Marine. Visit the 12th-17thC tower, from where there are excellent views of the town and French Navy vessels. There is also a harbour rampart walk.

MUSÉE DES BEAUX-ARTS 22 rue de la Traverse.
■ 1000-1145, 1400-1845 Wed.-Sat. & Mon., 1400-1845 Sun. ● Free.
*A balanced collection of 17th-18thC Dutch, Italian and French paintings, plus Manet, Utrillo and the Pont-Aven School (see **A-Z**).*

TOUR TANGUY & MUSÉE DE VIEUX BREST Rue de la Tour, near Pont de Recouvrance. ■ 1000-1200, 1400-1900 July & Aug.; 1400-1900 June & Sep., Sat. & Sun. (Oct.-May). ● Free.
In 16thC tower: 1st floor, pre-Revolution; 2nd floor, 19th-20thC history.

ÉGLISE ST. LOUIS Rue Étienne Dolet.
■ 0800-1200, 1400-1900.
Built in 1958, it is notable for its stained-glass windows and tapestries.

OCEANOPOLIS Port de Plaisance du Moulin Blanc, 4 km east of the chateau. ■ 1000-1900. ● 50F, 18-25s 45F.
Huge sophisticated aquarium with bookshops, boutiques, cinema and restaurants. The ideal 'sub-marine' resort!

CONSERVATOIRE BOTANIQUE NATIONAL DU STANGALARD 52 allée du Biot, 4 km east of the chateau.
■ 0900-1200, 1400-1730 Mon.-Fri., 1400-1730 Sat. & Sun. ● Gardens Free, hothouses 20F.
Europe's second-largest botanical gardens; over 1000 protected species.

LE MÉMORIAL FORT MONTBAREY Allée Bir-Hakeim.
■ 1400-1800 Wed.-Mon. ● 23F.
*A new museum showing Breton resistance to Nazi occupation during World War II (see **A-Z**).*

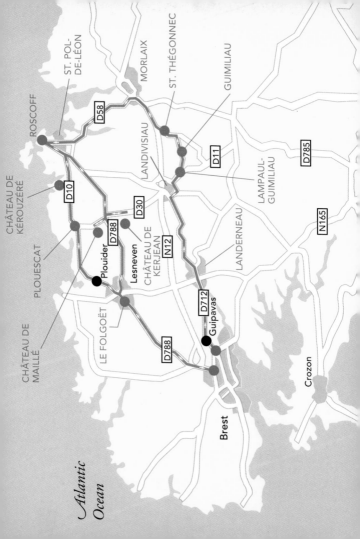

Excursion

A one-day excursion to parish closes, St. Pol-de-Léon and Le Folgoët.

Leave Brest on Rue de la Villeneuve, then take the D 712 through Guipavas.

20 km – Landerneau (pop: 15,500) has two interesting churches – 17thC St. Houardon, and 16thC St. Thomas de Cantorbery with an ossuary of 1635 nearby. In the wide river Elorn between the two main bridges are nesting boxes for swans and ducks, and Rue du Pont has old houses and the tourist office. La Duchesse Anne bistro, in a 17thC house in Pl. Général de Gaulle, has a good plat du jour, while the beflagged and popular Hôtel-Restaurant L'Amandier on the Rte de Brest offers four prix fixe menus. Continue 16 km east on the D 712.

36 km – Landivisiau. Pop: 8000. A busy market town with the good-value Hôtel-Restaurant de l'Avenue. The parish close (see **A-Z**) circuit now begins. There are 20 villages in an area of approximately 30 sq km. You should try to visit the most spectacular at Lampaul-Guimiliau, Guimiliau and St. Thégonnec which lie in a triangle to the southeast of Landivisiau. The D 111 and D 118 circuit of the three famous *enclos* is 18 km long. Join the N 12 east for 15 km.

79 km – Morlaix (see **A-Z**). A busy commercial town, twinned with Truro, at the mouth of the Baie de Morlaix. The rivers Jarlo and Queffleut join and flow underground for 600 m and reappear on the south side of the town. A huge viaduct crosses the town approach and the tourist office is situated almost underneath it. There are two churches of interest, and you should particularly note St. Matthew's life depicted in 14 large stained-glass windows in the Église de St. Mathieu. The Musée des Jacobins (see **BREST-MUSEUMS**) is also worth a visit. The town still has some traces of the Middle Ages in Grande Rue, Rue Ange-de-Guernisac, and venelles de Creou and au Son around the Église St. Melaine on the eastern slopes. Morlaix has five hotels, including Hôtel-Restaurant Europe, which serves *filets de sole poêlées au beurre d'eau-de-vie de cidre* – sounds irresistible! Take the D 58 north.

100 km – St. Pol-de-Léon (pop: 8000) is twinned with Penarth. St. Paul Aurelian's 12th-16thC cathedral is one of the finest in Brittany. Look out for St. Paul's bronze bell, brought to him by a fish, an 11thC water-stoup, Roman sarcophagus, 15thC rose windows, 16thC carved stalls

St. Thégonnec

Tour Tanguy & Château de Brest

and the gilded shrine with relics of the saint. Three hundred metres down the hill is the formidable fortified 14th-15thC Chapelle de Kreisker (0800-1200, 1400-1900; 10F) with its famous belfry, which served as a watchtower against invaders. Climb 170 steps to view the coastline. Also note the extraordinary 16thC wooden statue, *Christ aux Outrages*. Hôtel-Restaurant de France at 29 rue des Minimes has inexpensive meals. Continue 5 km north on the D 769.

105 km – Roscoff (see **A-Z**) is a ferry port situated by a large natural bay with two headlands. To the west are the 16thC Notre Dame de Kroaz-Batz and the large Charles Pérez aquarium (1000-1200, 1400-1800 June-Sep., 1400-1800 Oct.-May; 25F). The Chapelle de Ste Barbe and huge fish farms (*viviers*) are on the eastern Pointe de Bloscon. The fishing port provides lobsters for the many hotel-restaurants in the town. On leaving Roscoff there is a choice.

Either: Take the high road (D 10) via Château de Kérouzéré (1000-1200, 1400-1800 Mon.-Sat.; ring main gate bell, 15F), a fine 15thC castle with three huge towers and pepperpot turrets, Plouescat and its five good beaches, and Plouider to Le Folgoët.

Or: Take the low road, the D 788, which is slightly shorter unless you make detours north to Château de Maillé (1000-1200, 1400-1800 Tue.-Thu., mid June-Sep., tel: 98614468 to view), an elegant 17thC grey-slated manor house, and south to Château de Kerjean (0930-1200, 1400-1900 Wed.-Mon.; 25F), a 16thC fortress-chateau with moat, ramparts and fine furnishings, both on the D 30.

144 km – Le Folgoët (pop: 3000) is part of Lesneven and twinned with Carmarthen. The great Basilique de Notre Dame has several famous pardons (see **A-Z**) each year, particularly the 4th Sun. in July and the 1st weekend in Sep. Note the carved-granite 15thC rood screen, a porch with 13 Apostles, and the holy fountain at the back of the church. Inside, look for a small urn on a pillar presented by the Black Watch in 1937 containing *terre d'Écosse* to commemorate the battle of La Boisselle in 1915. Across the street is a 15thC manor house and pilgrim hostel which houses a small museum (1000-1200, 1400-1830 Mon.-Sat., 1400-1830 Sun., July-mid Sep.; 17F). From Le Folgoët it is 24 km on the D 788 back to Brest (168 km).

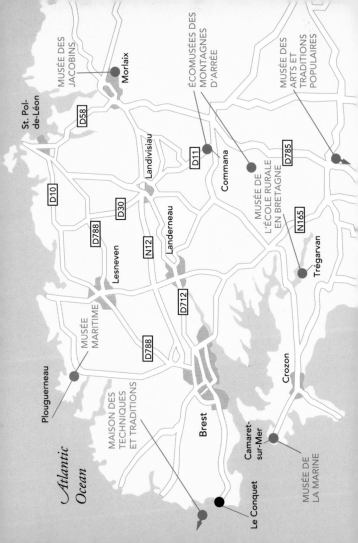

Atlantic Ocean

MUSÉE DES JACOBINS

Morlaix

St. Pol-de-Léon

ÉCOMUSÉES DES MONTAGNES D'ARRÉE

MUSÉE DES ARTS ET TRADITIONS POPULAIRES

D58

D11

Commana

MUSÉE DE L'ÉCOLE RURALE EN BRETAGNE

D785

Landivisiau

D10

D30

N12

Landerneau

N165

Lesneven

D788

Trégarvan

D712

D788

Plouguerneau

MUSÉE MARITIME

Crozon

MAISON DES TECHNIQUES ET TRADITIONS

Brest

Camaret-sur-Mer

MUSÉE DE LA MARINE

Le Conquet

Museums

MUSÉE DE LA MARINE
Tour Vauban, Camaret-sur-Mer, southwest of Brest. ■ 1000-1145, 1400-1845 July-Sep. ● 17F.
A naval museum, including displays on the history of the Camaret region.

ÉCOMUSÉES DES MONTAGNES D'ARRÉE
1. Moulin de Kerouat, Commana. 2. La Maison Cornec, St. Rivoal. East of Brest. ■ 1100-1900 July & Aug. ● 15F.
Two small rural-traditions museums situated 10 km apart in the Armorique (see A-Z) nature park.

MUSÉE DES ARTS ET TRADITIONS POPULAIRES
Pl. de la Mairie, Locronan, southeast of Brest.
■ 1030-1230, 1430-1830 mid June-Sep. ● 15F.
Displays of paintings, furnishings and costumes.

MUSÉE DES JACOBINS
Pl. des Jacobins, Morlaix, east of Brest.
■ 1000-1200, 1400-1800 Wed.-Mon. ● 20F.
History of the local Léon and Petit Trégor regions, as well as Breton sculptures, 19thC paintings and furniture in a Dominican convent. See BREST-EXCURSION.

MUSÉE MARITIME
Rte St. Michel, Plouguerneau, north of Brest.
■ 1000-1230, 1500-1930 mid June-mid Sep. ● 17F.
Local fishing traditions are shown by means of paintings, models and static displays.

MUSÉE DE L'ÉCOLE RURALE EN BRETAGNE
Ancienne École, Trégarvan, southeast of Brest. ■ 1000-1200, 1400-1830 July-mid Sep.; Sat. & Sun. (mid Sep.-mid July). ● 15F.
The history of Breton rural education housed in a 19thC school.

MAISON DES TECHNIQUES ET TRADITIONS
Île d'Ouessant, northwest of Brest. ■ 1100-1830 April-Sep. ● 16F.
An 18thC house displaying the fishermen's life style over the last three centuries.

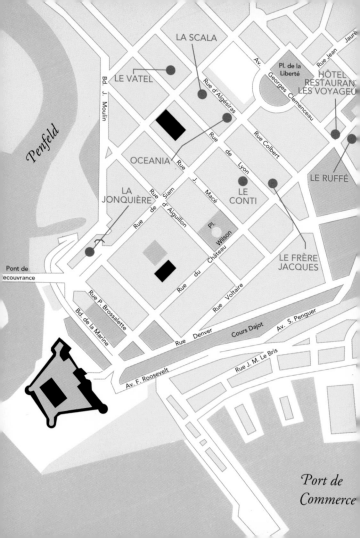

LA SCALA

LE VATEL

Rue d'Algésiras

Av. Georges Clemenceau

Pl. de la Liberté

Rue Jean Jaurè

HÔTEL
RESTAURAN
LES VOYAGEU

Bd. J. Moulin

Penfeld

OCEANIA

Rue de Lyon

Rue Colbert

LE RUFFÉ

LA JONQUIÈRE

Rue de Siam

Rue d'Aiguillon

Rue J. Macé

LE CONTI

Pl. Wilson

Rue du Château

LE FRÈRE
JACQUES

Pont de
ecouvrance

Rue Voltaire

Rue P. Brossalette

Bd. de la Marine

Rue Denver

Cours Dajot

Av. S. Penguer

Av. F. Roosevelt

Rue J. M. Le Bris

Port de
Commerce

Restaurants

LE FRÈRE JACQUES 15 bis rue de Lyon.
■ 1200-1400, 1930-2145 Mon.-Fri., 1930-2145 Sat. Closed July.
● Expensive.
Classic Breton meals by a top chef, i.e. Demoiselle de Loctudy.

HÔTEL-RESTAURANT LES VOYAGEURS
15 av. Georges Clemenceau. ■ ■ 1200-1400, 2000-2200 Tue.-Sat., 1200-1400 Sun. Closed mid July-mid Aug. ● Expensive.
Superb dishes and a good selection of wines. Has its own shellfish shop.

LE VATEL 23 rue Fautras.
■ 1200-1400, 1945-2200 Mon.-Fri., 1945-2200 Sat. Closed Aug.
● Expensive.
Good Breton cuisine and Nantais wines in a dark blue building.

OCEANIA Sofitel Hotel, 82 rue de Siam.
■ 1145-1415, 1930-2130. ● Moderate-Expensive.
Top-ranking modern hotel-restaurant with several menus.

LE CONTI Althea Hotel, 41 rue Emile Zola.
■ 1145-1415, 1900-2100. ● Moderate.
Large hotel-restaurant overlooking a small park with cherry trees.

LE RUFFÉ 1 rue Yves Collet.
■ 1200-1415, 1915-2100 Mon.-Sat. ● Moderate.
A small family-run restaurant. Try the salade de mer Ouessantine.

LA SCALA 30 rue d'Algésiras, at corner of Rue Kéréon.
■ 1200-1400, 1930-2115 Mon.-Sat. ● Moderate.
Small Italian restaurant near the new market with carpaccio meat dishes.

LA JONQUIÈRE 14 rue de Siam.
■ 1100-2200 Mon.-Sat. ● Inexpensive.
Trendy glacier-restaurant decorated in green and white. Three menus are available. Try the terrine de saumon à la crème et d'échalote. *Ice creams are served on the outside terrace.*

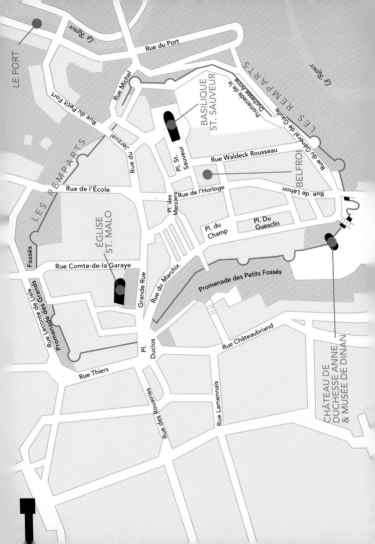

LE PORT

La Rance

Rue du Port

Rue Michel

Rue du Petit Fort

Rue Jerzual

Rue du Jerzual

LES REMPARTS

Rue de l'École

ÉGLISE ST. MALO

Rue Comte-de-la Garaye

Rue Leconte de l'Isle

Promenade des Grands

Fossés

Rue Thiers

Pl. Duclos

Grande Rue

Rue des Rouairies

Rue du Marchix

Pl. St. Sauveur

BASILIQUE ST. SAUVEUR

Promenade de la Duchesse Anne

Promenade du Général de Gaulle

LES REMPARTS

La Rance

Rue Waldeck Rousseau

Rue de l'Horloge

Pl. des Merciers

Pl. du Champ

Pl. Du Guesclin

BELFROI

Rue de Léhon

Promenade des Petits Fossés

Rue Châteaubriand

Rue Lamennais

CHÂTEAU DE DUCHESSE ANNE & MUSÉE DE DINAN

VIEILLE VILLE *See* DINAN-WALK.

CHÂTEAU DE DUCHESSE ANNE & MUSÉE DE DINAN
Porte du Guichet. ■ 0900-1200, 1400-1900 Wed.-Mon. (Mar.-Oct.),
1400-1900 Nov.-Feb. ● 20F.
The enormous oval-shaped 14thC Tour Coetquen houses this major
museum, with displays of local crafts, religious art, costumes and
Dinan's history. Also see High Constable's room, chapel and armoury.

LES REMPARTS
Five hundred metres of 13thC ramparts between Tour Ste Catherine and
Promenade de la Duchesse Anne, plus, in clockwise rotation, Porte du
Jerzual, Tour du Sillon, Tour Penthièvre, Porte St. Louis, Tour Coetquen
(see above), Porte du Guichet, donjon (keep of chateau), Tour du
Connétable, Tour de Beaufort, Porte de Brest, Tour St. Julien, Tour de
Lesquen, Tour Beaumanoir, Porte St. Malo and Tour du Gouverneur.

BELFROI Rue de l'Horloge.
■ 1045-1315, 1500-1800 Mon.-Sat., 1500-1800 Sun. ● 17F.
15th-17thC, 30 m-high clock tower with 158 steps to the top for superb
panoramas.

BASILIQUE ST. SAUVEUR Pl. St. Sauveur, near Jardin Anglais.
■ 0800-1200, 1400-1900.
Features a 12thC façade, 17thC three-tiered steeple, Du Guesclin's (see
A-Z) heart in the north chapel, two-laddered pulpit and unusual stained-
glass windows of a dozen saints, including Roche, Crispin and Clement.

ÉGLISE ST. MALO Grande Rue.
■ 0800-1900.
A huge Gothic church completed in 1490, with a notable chancel and
choir, and two-laddered pulpit. The unusual historical stained-glass win-
dows, installed in the 1920s, are also of interest.

LE PORT
Small marina on the river Rance offering cruises to St. Malo and Dinard.

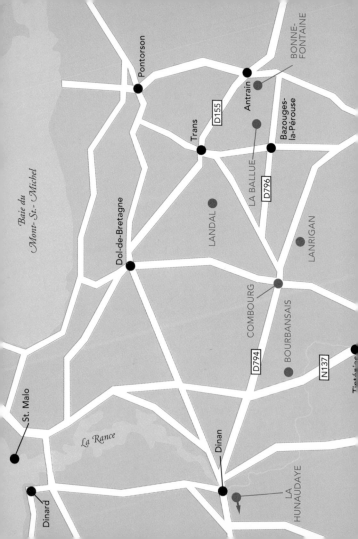

Baie du
Mont-St.-Michel

La Rance

Pontorson

Trans

D155

Antrain

BONNE-
FONTAINE

Bazouges-
la-Pérouse

LA BALLUE

D796

LANRIGAN

Dol-de-Bretagne

LANDAL

COMBOURG

BOURBANSAIS

D794

N137

Tintiniac

St. Malo

Dinard

Dinan

LA
HUNAUDAYE

Castles & Chateaux

COMBOURG 23 rue des Princes, 24 km east on the D 974.
■ 1400-1730 Wed.-Mon. (April-Oct.). ● 30F.
*Set among tall trees, this 11th-15thC fortress with towers, ramparts and a chapel, dominates the town. The drawing room and archives have mementoes of Chateaubriand's (see **A-Z**) time spent here in the 18thC.*

LA BALLUE Bazouges-la-Pérouse, 40 km east off the D 796.
■ 1000-1900 mid April-mid Oct. ● Grounds only 15F.
*A fine rose-granite chateau which was the HQ of the Chouans (see **A-Z**) rebels in 1793. Set in gardens with over 500 trees, it inspired Victor Hugo, Balzac and Musset.*

BONNE-FONTAINE Antrain, 50 km east off the N 175.
■ 1000-1800 Mon.-Sat. (April-Oct.). ● Grounds only 17F.
15th-16thC Loire-style chateau in woodlands and park, with elegant turrets, windows and façade.

LANDAL Broualan, 40 km east off the N 795.
■ 1000-1200, 1400-1700. ● Grounds only, Free.
Rather sad 15thC feudal castle in woodland near a lake, with four round towers and a courtyard.

LANRIGAN Combourg, 29 km east on the D 794.
■ 1000-1200, 1400-1700 Wed.-Fri. (June-Aug.). ● Grounds only 15F.
Charming Loire-style 15th-16thC small chateau near a lake, with tower and galleries.

BOURBANSAIS Pleugueneuc, 12 km southeast off the N 137.
■ Chateau 1400-1800. Zoo & gardens 1200-1800. ● Joint ticket 40F.
1583 Loire-style chateau in large park. Well-furnished with tapestries and porcelain.

LA HUNAUDAYE Plédéliac, 26 km west off the D 16.
■ 1000-1200, 1400-1700 July & Aug.; Sun. (April-June & Sep.). ● 15F.
*13thC ruined, but renovated, pentagon-shaped castle with keep, moat and courtyard. See **DINAN-EXCURSION**.*

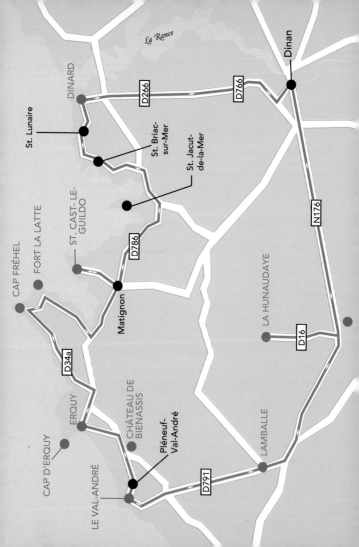

Excursion

A one-day excursion to Lamballe and St. Cast-le-Guildo.

Head west on the D 766 for St. Brieuc and after 4 km join the N 176 for 17 km to the small town of Jugon-les-Lacs, an ideal open-air holiday resort with a huge lake, sailing and riding schools, and good fishing and bathing. La Hunaudaye (see **DINAN-CASTLES & CHATEAUX**) lies 10 km north via the D 16. Keep on the N 176 for 18 km.

39 km – Lamballe (pop: 5000) is situated on a hill with the river Gouessant circling the main sights – the Gothic collegiate church of Notre Dame, the Musée Mathurin Méheut and Musée de Vieux Lamballe (see **ST. BRIEUC-MUSEUMS**) and the *haras national*. This equine stud is open for viewing the stallions, dressage riding school and stables (1400-1630 Mon.-Sat., 1000-1200, 1400-1630 Sun., mid July-mid Sep.; Free). Take the D 791 due north for 11 km, then the D 786 for 5 km.

55 km – Le Val-André is one of the best resorts in Brittany. There is a fine sandy beach and good cliff-top walks. The Hôtel-Restaurant de la Mer has superb *nouvelle cuisine* and good-value rooms. Continue east on the D 786 through Pléneuf-Val-André and 6 km on the right is the 15th-17thC fortified Château de Bienassis (see **ST. BRIEUC-CASTLES & CHATEAUX**). Follow the D 786 back towards the coast at Erquy (pop: 3500), a fishing port with seven beaches within easy reach, and Cap d'Erquy, reached by a gentle walk. Head inland for 5 km then take the D 34a past several golden beaches, including Sables d'Or-les-Pins and Pléherel, to Cap Fréhel, from where there are extensive views. The lighthouse (see **A-Z**) is open for visits and the GR 34 (see **Walks**) takes you east towards Fort la Latte (see **ST. BRIEUC-CASTLES & CHATEAUX**), although the minor road takes you to within 600 m, from where you pass a solitary menhir to get to the lonely castle. Follow the minor coastal road, the D 16a/D 16, to rejoin the D 786 and in Matignon turn left on the D 13 for 6 km.

99 km – St. Cast-le-Guildo (pop: 3300) is a popular resort with beaches and a fishing port set between two attractive headlands – Pointe de St. Cast and Pointe de la Garde. Continue south past Pen-Guen Plage to rejoin the D 786. For the next 22 km, pass through a number of resorts, including St. Jacut-de-la-Mer and St. Briac-sur-Mer, to St. Lunaire and Dinard (see **A-Z**). Return to Dinan on the D 266 and D 766.

Dinan

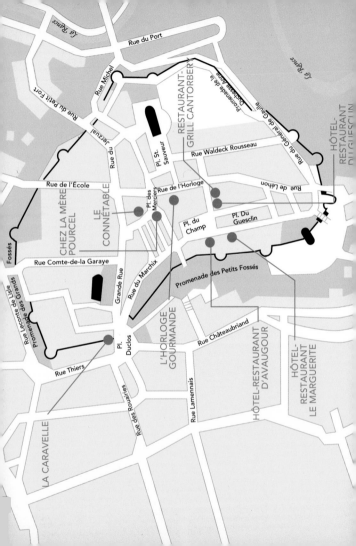

Restaurants

HÔTEL-RESTAURANT D'AVAUGOUR 1 pl. du Champ.
■ 1200-1400, 2000-2145. Closed Mon. in winter. ● Expensive.
In summer dine in a garden overlooking the ramparts. Afternoon salon de thé from 1600. Noted for its dorade poêlée à l'estragon frais à la provençale (sea bream with tarragon).

LA CARAVELLE 14 pl. Duclos.
■ 1200-1400, 1945-2145. Closed Oct. ● Moderate-Expensive.
Good-value prix fixe lunch but expensive à la carte dinner.

CHEZ LA MÈRE POURCEL 3 pl. des Merciers. ■ 1200-1400, 1930-2130 Tue.-Sat., 1200-1400 Sun. Closed Jan. & Feb. ● Moderate.
High-class French cuisine served in a 15thC house with an unusual staircase. Try the minute de saumon parfumée à l'orange.

HÔTEL-RESTAURANT LE MARGUERITE 27 pl. Du Guesclin.
■ 1200-1345, 1945-2145. ● Moderate.
An assortment of stuffed shellfish is a speciality here. The restaurant is in the house where Jean Cordelier, a local hero, lived.

HÔTEL-RESTAURANT DU GUESCLIN 9 rue Ste Claire.
■ 1200-1400, 1930-2130. ● Moderate.
Note the model sailing ships on the walls. Try the trout in almonds.

RESTAURANT-GRILL CANTORBERY 6 rue Ste Claire.
■ 1145-1415, 1930-2130. ● Moderate.
Fish and meat dishes are grilled over wood fires.

L'HORLOGE GOURMANDE Passage de l'Horloge.
■ 1145-1400, 1930-2130. ● Inexpensive.
A quiet courtyard restaurant serving grills, salads and galettes.

LE CONNÉTABLE 1 rue de l'Apport.
■ 1130-2130. ● Inexpensive.
The oldest creperie in Dinan, in a 15thC house. Try a banana Chantilly crepe (see Food) for dessert, washed down with local cider.

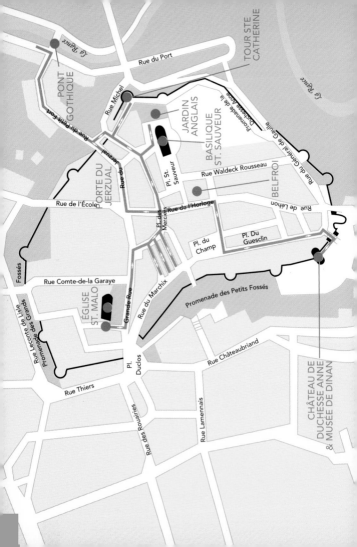

Walk

Duration: 2 hr 30 min.

The old town of Dinan is surrounded by 3 km of ramparts with 15 towers and gates, and the chateau. Within is a complex of attractive nar-
row cobbled streets in which are many medieval half-timbered houses
which once belonged to prosperous guild merchants.

The Église St. Malo (see **DINAN-
ATTRACTIONS**) is in Grande Rue,
which leads to Pl. des Cordeliers.
Chez La Mère Pourcel (see **DINAN-
RESTAURANTS**) occupies a fine 15thC
half-timbered house near the arcade
of the Cordeliers' monastery gate-
way. The large Ancien Couvent des
Cordeliers (now a school), with
15thC cloisters, courtyard and pepperpot towers, is 100 m east of the
Église St. Malo.

Adjoining is Rue de l'Apport, with
houses on pillars (à porche) with
high casement windows overlooking
the street or with gabled upper
storeys. To the right (west) are a tan-
gle of intriguing lanes (Rue du Petit-
Pain, Rue de la Mittrie, Rue de la
Cordonnerie). The fish caught in the
river Rance were originally marketed
here. The Ancien Hôtel Beaumanoir,
with its 16thC tower, staircase and
Renaissance doorway, is in Rue
Haute-Voie, 50 m to the east.

The northeast sector of the town is
more difficult! Rue du Jerzual, with its 15th-16thC shops, the subject of
paintings by Corot and many other artisans, slopes steeply down for
600 m through the Porte du Jerzual, along Rue du Petit Fort (the Maison
du Gouverneur at No. 24 houses a tapestry artisan) to the river, the port
(see **DINAN-ATTRACTIONS**) and the Pont Gothique. There are half a

dozen excellent restaurants and creperies – including Les Merveilles des Mer and Relais des Corsairs, both on Rue du Quai – to sustain you for the return walk uphill. To your left on the way back, Rue Michel and Rue du Rempart lead to the Tour Ste Catherine with stunning views of the river, port and bridge, ramparts, the Jardin Anglais (where the large trees are individually titled) and the Basilique St. Sauveur. It is then 200 m back into the centre of town to Rue de l'Horloge. The tourist office is in the most attractive house, the 1559 Hôtel Kératry. Just to the right is the 16thC Maison du Gisant, with a headless sculpted man, and the 15thC clock tower (Belfroi – see **DINAN-ATTRACTIONS**) and boutique courtyard. Rue Ste Claire leads to Pl. du Champ (now a major car park but once the tilt-ing and jousting yards). Du Guesclin (see **A-Z**), the scourge of the English at the beginning of the Hundred Years' War, fought and beat Thomas de Cantorbery here in 1359 with decisive military and romantic results. The future Constable of France married a pretty local girl and the English knight was disgraced!

The chateau and museum (see **DINAN-ATTRACTIONS**) are now 300 m south, and two peaceful walks with views are just west (Promenade des Petits Fossés) and 400 m east (Promenade de la Duchesse Anne).

POINTE DE LA MALOUINE

Rue des Marettes

Bd. Albert   Rue Lacroix

PLAGE DE L'ÉCLUSE

Rue de St. - Énogat

Rue Pionnière

PALAIS DES CONGRÈS

Bd. Wilson

Av.

Édouard VII

Rue de la Gare

Rue de la Corbinais

Bd. Féart

Av. George V

PROMENADE DU CLAIR DE LUNE

MUSÉE MARITIME ET L'AQUARIUM

Rue Pichot

MUSÉE DU SITE ET DE LA VIE BALNÉAIRE

Baie du Prieuré

Bd. de la Libération

Plage du Prieuré

Rue Gouyon Matignon

Av. de la Vicomté

USINE MARÉMOTRICE DE LA RANCE

PROMENADE DU CLAIR DE LUNE
A promenade, 1.5 km in length, from Plage du Prieuré towards Pointe du Moulinet, with superb views of St. Malo, the local marina and nearby islands. Also the venue for music (2130 July-Sep.) and son et lumière (see A-Z).

PLAGE DE L'ÉCLUSE
A gorgeous silver-sand beach between Pointe de la Malouine and Pointe du Moulinet. There is a pleasant promenade which passes an open-air piscine in the rocks, an indoor Olympic-size swimming pool (1000-1300, 1500-2000; 23F), the Palais des Congrès (see below) and the casino.

POINTE DE LA MALOUINE
A headland with superb views towards Cap Fréhel, St. Malo and the Rance dam (see below). Note the Edwardian villas set amid Riviera-style trees (palm, tamarisk, fig) and exotic gardens.

MUSÉE DU SITE ET DE LA VIE BALNÉAIRE 12 rue des
Françaises Libres. ■ 1400-1800 Tue.-Sun. (mid May-Oct.). ● 25F.
An interesting collection with many themes – archaeology, architecture, traditional trades and the historical development of this elegant spa which attracted the rich, famous and noble families of the belle époque.

MUSÉE MARITIME ET L'AQUARIUM 17 av. George V.
■ 1000-1200, 1400-1830 mid May-mid Sep. ● Joint ticket 20F.
Oceanology research by J.-B. Charcor; 100 fish species in 24 huge tanks.

PALAIS DES CONGRÈS Rue Coppinger.
A huge cultural complex which hosts theatre, opera, exhibitions, concerts, films, conferences and much more.

USINE MARÉMOTRICE DE LA RANCE 4 km southeast on the
D 168. ■ 0830-2000. ● Free.
30 min visits to see the hydro-electric plant inside the 750 m dam which harnesses tidal power to generate electricity.

Bd. Albert Lacroix

Rue des Marettes

LA PRÉSIDENCE

Plage de l'Écluse

LA COQUILLE

Rue de St. - Énogat

Rue Pionnière

Bd. Wilson

HÔTEL-RESTAURA LES DUNE

Av. Édouard VII

HÔTEL-RESTAURANT ALTAIR

LE TREZEN

GEORGE V

Av. George V

HÔTEL-RESTAURANT PRINTANIA

Rue de la Gare

Rue de la Corbinais

Bd. Féart

HÔTEL-RESTAURANT LES ALIZES

Rue Pichot

Bd. de la Libération

Plage du Prieuré

Baie du Prieuré

Rue Gouyon Matignon

Av. de la Vicomté

Restaurants

LA COQUILLE Hôtel Roche Corneille, 4 rue Georges Clemenceau.
■ 1200-1415, 1945-2145 Tue.-Sun. Closed mid Oct.-mid Mar.
● Expensive.
The large 1st-floor glass-enclosed terrace offers excellent shellfish, such as pièce de saumon poêlée aux huitres chaudes (salmon with oysters).

GEORGE V Le Grand Hôtel, 46 av. George V.
■ 1200-1400, 1900-2230. Closed Mar. ● Expensive.
Traditional carte gastronomique in appropriately grand surroundings.

HOTEL-RESTAURANT ALTAIR 18 bd. Féart. ■ 1200-1400 Sun.-Tue. & Thu., 1915-2115 Mon., Tue. & Thu. ● Moderate.
In a tall Victorian building. Sip your apéritif on a terrace among the palms. The oysters in cream are recommended.

LA PRÉSIDENCE 29 bd. Wilson.
■ 1200-1400, 1930-2130 Fri.-Wed. ● Moderate.
Small, pink-coloured restaurant serving grilled fish and meat dishes.

LE TREZEN Hôtel La Plage, 3 bd. Féart.
■ 1200-1400, 1945-2200. Closed Feb. & Mar. ● Moderate.
Try jambonette de lapin aux grosses crevettes (rabbit and prawns). There are views over the gardens.

HÔTEL-RESTAURANT LES ALIZES 9 rue des Mimosas.
■ 1200-1415 Thu.-Tue., 1930-2100 Mon., Tue., Thu.-Sat. ● Moderate.
Smoked salmon is the house speciality at this restaurant, situated in a corner block near the station.

HÔTEL-RESTAURANT PRINTANIA 5 av. George V.
■ 1200-1415 Thu.-Tue., 1930-2100 Mon., Tue., Thu., Sat. ● Moderate.
Fish dishes and regional cuisine served in a restaurant near the marina.

HÔTEL-RESTAURANT LES DUNES 5 rue Georges Clemenceau.
■ 1200-1400, 1945-2145. Closed Oct.-May. ● Moderate.
A pleasant garden terrace forms this restaurant's dining area.

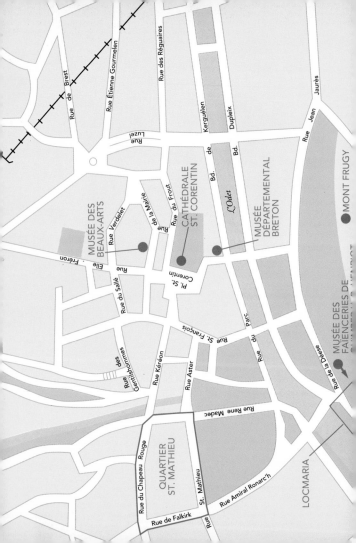

VIEILLE VILLE *See* QUIMPER-WALK.

CATHÉDRALE ST. CORENTIN Pl. St. Corentin.
■ 0830-1900. Closed Sun. pm.
*13th-15thC with 19thC steeples; fine 15thC stained-glass windows, plus chapels, tombs, statues, frescoes and King Gradlon (see **A-Z**) on horse-back on the roof!*

MUSÉE DES BEAUX-ARTS 40 pl. St. Corentin.
■ 0930-1200, 1330-1900 Wed.-Mon. Closed Jan. ● 30F.
*Pont-Aven School (see **A-Z**), plus Rubens, Corot, Picasso and local Breton artists. The museum also has Max Jacob drawings.*

MUSÉE DÉPARTEMENTAL BRETON 1 rue du Roi Gradlon.
■ 0900-1200, 1400-1900 Tue.-Fri., 1400-1900 Sat. & Sun. ● 25F.
Renovated museum of Breton folklore, with displays of furniture, wood-en statues, archaeology and pottery.

QUARTIER ST. MATHIEU 300 m west of the cathedral.
Old houses in the streets around the 17thC Église St. Mathieu, including Rue St. Mathieu and Pl. Terre-aux-Ducs.

LOCMARIA Southwest of the town centre.
Suburb with the 15thC Notre Dame de Locmaria church and two impor-tant faïence makers, Henriot (see below) and Kéraluc. Vedette trips (1.5 hr) go south to Bénodet; embark on the north bank.

MUSÉE DES FAÏENCERIES DE QUIMPER H. B. HENRIOT
Allées Locmaria.
■ 1000-1200, 1400-1800 Mon.-Fri. ● 20F.
Three centuries of Quimper faïence (tin-glazed earthenware) displayed in a museum linked with the Henriot firm.

MONT FRUGY On south bank of the river.
Hillside gardens with panoramic views. It is a 30 min walk from Pl. de la Résistance to the belvedere.

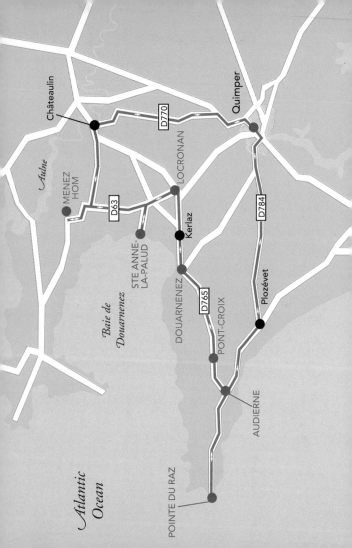

Excursion 1

A one-day excursion to Douarnenez, Locronan and Menez Hom.

Leave Quimper westwards on the D 765 and after 5 km fork left on the D 784 for 19 km. Continue for 10 km beyond Plozévet.

34 km – Audierne. Pop: 3000. At the mouth of the river Goyen, Audierne is an attractive resort with a working fishing port and marina, from where vedettes leave for the Île de Sein (see **Islands**). There are 15 beaches in the area, many small and well worth exploring. Continuing the 15 km to the Pointe du Raz will show you the genuine unspoilt Brittany. Hamlets of small whitewashed houses with slate roofs, road-side calvaries, spotlessly clean countryside and at the end of the world – 'finis-terre' – savage cliffs defying the Atlantic swell. Return to Audierne and keep on the D 765 past several fish farms where crabs and lobsters with an uncertain future are kept in large tanks. Pont-Croix (pop: 1900) is a quiet town. In a side street littered with flowers is the magnificent Église Notre Dame de Roscidon, mainly 13thC with a fine belfry and porch. A major pardon (see **A-Z**) takes place on 15 Aug.

86 km – Douarnenez (pop: 18,000) has a smart little resort, Tréboul-plage, Île Tristan and several ports from where vedettes sail. It is a lively town with an old quarter around the marketplace and the churches of St. Michel and Ste Hélène. A great centre of Breton folklore and Celtic legends (see **Tristan & Isolde**), there are many fêtes and pardons throughout the summer. The early-morning fish auction (see **A-Z**) is a typical Breton sight. Take the D 7 eastwards for 10 km past Kerlaz.

96 km – Locronan (see **A-Z**) is an incomparable Renaissance village and 1995 sees the next Grande Troménie pardon. Drive north on the D 63 for 5 km and at Plonévez-Porzay make a detour westwards to see the lonely but famous 19thC chapel of Ste Anne-la-Palud, deserted for most of the year, but on the last Sun. of Aug. the scene of the most pic-turesque pardon in Brittany. Go northwards on the D 61 to Ploéven, the D 63 to Plomodiern, then follow the D 47 and D 83.

118 km – Menez Hom. Park your car and walk up the gentle slopes to the 330 m peak, which will give you unrivalled views of the Parc Naturel Régional d'Armorique (see **A-Z**), Brest in the distance and the bay of Douarnenez. Return to Quimper via the D 887 east to Châteaulin, and southwards on the D 770.

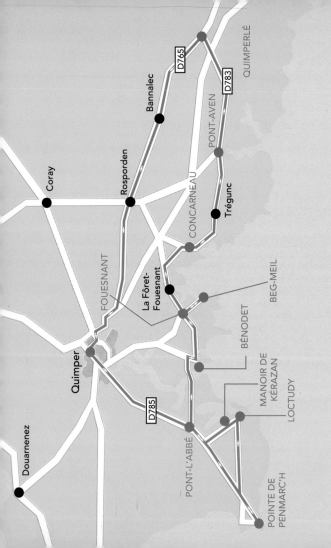

QUIMPERLÉ

D765

Bannalec

Coray

Rosporden

PONT-AVEN

D783

CONCARNEAU

Trégunc

FOUESNANT

La Fôret-Fouesnant

BEG-MEIL

BÉNODET

Quimper

MANOIR DE KÉRAZAN

LOCTUDY

Douarnenez

D785

PONT-L'ABBÉ

POINTE DE PENMARC'H

A one- or two-day excursion to Pont-l'Abbé, Concarneau, Pont-Aven and Quimperlé.

Take the D 785 southwest out of Quimper.
20 km – Pont-l'Abbé. Pop: 7700. A quiet little port with the Château-Musée Bigouden (see **QUIMPER-MUSEUMS**) by a lake, and the 14thC abbey of Notre Dame des Carmes with notable 15thC stained-glass windows, where there is a mid-July pardon (see **A-Z**). A 14 km drive southwest on the D 785 brings you to the Pointe de Penmarc'h with menhirs, chapels and calvaries. Return on the D 53 to Loctudy (pop: 3600) and the fine Manoir de Kérazan (1100-1900 July & Aug., 1300-1900 Wed.-Mon., April-June & Sep.; 35F), a pepperpot-roofed manor house which is a combination of art gallery and Breton 'Kew Gardens', off the D 2. Back in Pont-l'Abbé go eastwards on the D 44.
68 km – Bénodet (pop: 2300) is a popular resort with beaches galore, a casino, large marina and vedettes up the river Odet. There are 12 hotels and from the Hôtel-Restaurant Gwel Kaer, 3 av. de la Plage, you can watch the vedettes sail to the Îles de Glénan (see **Islands**). The D 44 continues to the east to Fouesnant (pop: 5500) which has a 12th-18thC church, a pardon at the end of July and the best cider in Brittany (so they claim!). To the south is Beg-Meil, another small resort amid dunes and pine trees. At La Forêt-Fouesnant join the D 783.
100 km – Concarneau (see **A-Z**). Just off the quayside of the large fishing port is the granite-walled medieval village, the Ville Close. It is absolutely beautiful and very photogenic, but a tourist trap in the season. Shaped like a horseshoe, the main street, Rue Vauban, about 400 m in length, harbours the Musée de la Pêche (see **QUIMPER-MUSEUMS**), a curious fish-shell museum, a church, half a dozen restaurants and a score of souvenir shops. A walk around the ramparts is recommended and the views are terrific. On your way out note the huge sundial near the main gate. A restaurant to try in the Ville Close is Le Galion, 15 rue St. Guénolé, and in the main town La Gallandière, 3 pl. Général de Gaulle, where the speciality is *langoustines grillées*. The Marinarium du Collège de France (see **QUIMPER-MUSEUMS**), an ultramodern aquarium, is on Quai de la Croix near the marina, and the vedette excursions leave for Beg-Meil, Bénodet and the Îles de Glénan. Twinned with

Penzance, Concarneau should be visited preferably in spring or autumn, and if you are making an overnight stay try to get up early to see the fish auction (see **A-Z**). Keep east on the D 873 through Trégunc.

114 km – Pont-Aven. Pop: 3300. Another beautiful tourist trap! The tidal river Aven runs through the little town. The Hôstellerie Moulin de Rosmadel with water wheels and tumbling water amid trees and shrubs is in a lovely setting. On the opposite side of the road is the most attractive stone-built WC in Brittany, located over the river! The Pont-Aven School (see **A-Z**) museum, the Musée de Gauguin (see **QUIMPER-MUSEUMS**), is next to the Hôtel de Ville in the triangular main square. A dozen galleries will tempt you with modern art, while *fabrique artisanale de poupées* (dolls) and *galettes de Pont-Aven* (cakes) make unusual presents. Before you leave, walk 500 m along Rue du Pont parallel to the river, to see the views, ships and more galleries and exhibitions. Drive east another 14 km on the D 783 via Riec-sur-Bélon.

128 km – Quimperlé (see **A-Z**) is bisected by the rivers Isole and Ellé which join to create the Laïta. The two halves of the town face each other, and both have interesting churches. The 12thC Ste Croix to the east has a crypt and apse, and Notre Dame de l'Assomption on the west bank is 13th-15thC. The Musée d'Histoire Locale et Traditions Bretonne (1000-1200, 1400-1800 July & Aug.; 18F) is in the Hôtel des Archeurs (1470) and depicts Quimperlé's history and folklore, as well as the writer La Villemarque's works. Twinned with Liskeard, Quimperlé is a peaceful inland town of some charm with a score of medieval houses on the Bremond d'Ars and Rue Dom Morice. The restaurant Le Rialto is perched on stilts over the river Isole, and La Vache Enragée, 3 rue Jacques Cartier (halfway up the hill on the west side) offers *l'onglet à l'échalote* (beef with shallots). Return to Quimper either on the N 165 or by the more leisurely D 765 through Bannalec and Rosporden.

Quimper

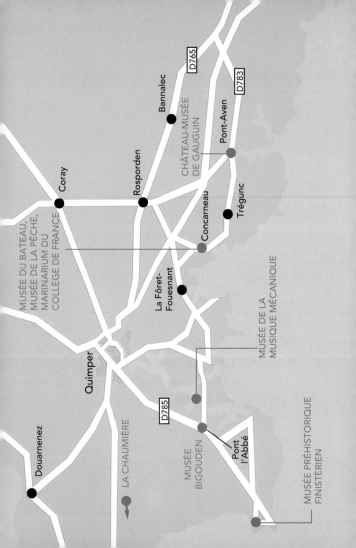

Bannalec

D765

D783

Pont-Aven

CHÂTEAU-MUSÉE
DE GAUGUIN

Coray

Rosporden

Trégunc

Concarneau

MUSÉE DU BATEAU,
MUSÉE DE LA PÊCHE,
MARINARIUM DU
COLLÈGE DE FRANCE

La Fôret-
Fouesnant

MUSÉE DE LA
MUSIQUE MÉCANIQUE

Quimper

Douarnenez

D785

MUSÉE
BIGOUDEN

Pont
l'Abbé

LA CHAUMIÈRE

MUSÉE PRÉHISTORIQUE
FINISTÉRIEN

Museums

LA CHAUMIÈRE Rue de la Plage, Audierne, west of Quimper.
■ 0830-1130, 1400-1830 July & Aug., 0900-1200, 1400-1800 Mon.-Thu. (Sep.-June). ● 25F.
16th-18thC Breton furnishings and interiors in a thatched cottage.

MUSÉE DE LA MUSIQUE MÉCANIQUE Combrit, southwest of Quimper. ■ 1200-1800 mid June-mid Sep. ● 20F.
Every kind of mechanical musical instrument, including street hurdy-gurdies, organs and pianos.

MUSÉE DE LA PÊCHE Rue Vauban, Ville Close, Concarneau.
■ 1000-1800 July & Aug., 1000-1200, 1430-1800 Sep.-June. ● 30F.
In old arsenal: shows the history of the port and houses ancient boats and an aquarium. See **QUIMPER-EXCURSION 2**.

MARINARIUM DU COLLÈGE DE FRANCE Quai de la Croix, Concarneau. ■ 1000-1200, 1400-1800 June-Sep. ● 17F.
A fish museum and aquarium, which also has flora and fauna displays. See **QUIMPER-EXCURSION 2**.

MUSÉE DU BATEAU Pl. de l'Enfer, Concarneau.
■ 1000-1200, 1400-1800 April-Sep. ● 17F.
A collection of fishing boats from the sardine and tunny fleets.

CHÂTEAU-MUSÉE DE GAUGUIN Pl. de l'Hotel de Ville, Pont-Aven, southeast of Quimper. ■ 1000-1200, 1400-1800 April-Sep. ● 30F.
Temporary Pont-Aven School exhibitions. See **QUIMPER-EXCURSION 2**.

MUSÉE BIGOUDEN Pont-l'Abbé, southwest of Quimper.
■ 1000-1200, 1400-1800 Mon.-Sat. (June-Sep.). ● 20F.
Folklore, costumes and furnishing displays. See **QUIMPER-EXCURSION 2**.

MUSÉE PRÉHISTORIQUE FINISTÈRIEN, St. Guénolé, southwest of Quimper. ■ 1000-1200, 1400-1800 Mon. & Wed.-Sat., 1400-1800 Sun. (June-Sep.). ● 20F.
Finds from the region dating from the Stone Age to Gallo-Roman times.

LE CAPUCIN GOURMAND

Rue des Réguaires

HÔTEL-RESTAURANT
LA TOUR D'AUVERGNE

Rue Étienne Gourmelen

Rue de Brest

Kerguélen

Duplex

Rue Luzel

L'AMBROISIE

Rue Jean Jaurès

Bd. de

Bd.

L'Odet

LA PARISIENNE

Rue de la Mairie

Rue Verdelet

AU CHASSE-MARÉE

Rue du Frout

Rue Elie Fréron

Pl. St. Corentin

LE CLOS
DE LA
TOURBIE

Rue du Sallé

LE GRAND CAFÉ
DE BRETAGNE

LA JONQUIÈRE

LE JARDIN
D'ÉTÉ

Rue des Gentilshommes

Rue Kéréon

Rue St. François

Rue du Parc

Rue de la Déesse

Rue Aster

Rue René Madec

Rue du Chapeau Rouge

St. Mathieu

Rue de Falkirk

Rue Amiral Ronarc'h

Restaurants

LE CAPUCIN GOURMAND 29 rue des Réguaires.
■ 1200-1330, 2000-2130 Mon.-Fri., 2000-2130 Sat. ● Expensive.
Smart and elegant restaurant with top-class international cuisine.

HOTEL-RESTAURANT LA TOUR D'AUVERGNE 13 rue des
Réguaires. ■ 1200-1400, 1945-2130 May-Sep. ● Expensive.
Breton specialities, a fine seafood choice and two prix fixe menus.

LA PARISIENNE 13 rue Jean Jaurès.
■ 1200-1330, 1945-2115 Mon.-Sat. Closed mid July-Aug. ● Expensive.
Very popular with Quimper businessmen for its haute cuisine.

L'AMBROISIE 49 rue Elie Fréron.
■ 1200-1400, 2000-2130. ● Expensive.
Breton seafood specialities. Also try the Muscadet and Gros-Plant wines.

LE JARDIN D'ÉTÉ 15 rue du Sallé.
■ 1200-1400, 2000-2200. Closed Tue. out of season. ● Moderate.
*Small, smart courtyard restaurant which is proud of its perfumed
cheeses. Salon de thé from 1430-1830 with a choice of 20 blends of tea.*

LE GRAND CAFÉ DE BRETAGNE 18 rue du Parc.
■ 1200-1430, 2000-2300. Closed Sun. out of season. ● Moderate.
Large cheerful brasserie overlooking the river. Noted for its patisserie.

LE CLOS DE LA TOURBIE 41 rue Elie Fréron.
■ 1200-1415, 1930-2130 Mon.-Sat. ● Moderate.
A small, elegant restaurant. The speciality fish dish is recommended.

AU CHASSE-MARÉE 10 rue du Guéodet.
■ 1200-1400, 1930-2130 Mon.-Sat. ● Inexpensive.
Tiny fish restaurant near the cathedral with a corsair tavern sign outside.

LA JONQUIÈRE Halles St. François.
■ 1200-1500, 2000-2300. ● Inexpensive.
*A wide choice of fish and meat dishes, as well as crepes (see **Food**).*

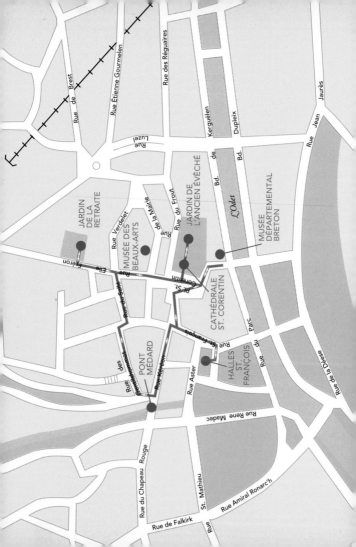

Duration: 2-3 hr.
Start at the covered market, Halles St. François, which has recently
been rebuilt. Turn left on Rue de la Grandière for 50 m. On the corner
to the right is a view of Mont Frugy. Turn left on Rue St. François, then
go left on Rue Kéréon, with a view back to the cathedral, and between
old corbelled houses to Pont Médard, from where there are views of
the little river Steir as it joins the main river Odet. Turn sharp right into
Rue des Gentilshommes, which has several 17thC half-timbered houses. On a wall at the end is a ceramic plaque with two fine swashbuck-
ling cavaliers (*gentilshommes*). Immediately turn left on Rue du Sallé
and look at Nos 16, 17 and 6. Walk through the little square, Pl. au
Beurre, where salted butter (*sallé*) was originally scooped with wooden
spoons into large earthenware jars. Rue Elie Fréron (named after an
18thC literary critic) was once called Rue Obscure because the bay
windows on both sides of the street almost touched in the middle. Walk
up the hill to the left and explore the beautiful Jardin de la Retraite
(0800-1900) with its formal rose gardens, banana and palm trees, and
the remains of ramparts and watchtowers, then head back down the
hill into the main square. Pl. St. Corentin houses the Hôtel de Ville,
Musée des Beaux-Arts (see **QUIMPER-ATTRACTIONS**) and the King
Gradlon (see **A-Z**) equestrian statue aloft between the two cathedral
towers. The Cathédrale St. Corentin (see **QUIMPER-ATTRACTIONS**) has
beautiful 15thC stained-glass windows, a chapel housing the miraculous Trois Gouttes de Sang, the Lady (or Victor) chapel which commemorates the 11thC victory by the Earl of Cornwall over the Duke of
Brittany, the grand organ of 1643 built by Robert Dallam, the delicate
sculpture of the main doors, frescoes of an 18thC entombment, and
15thC tombs, making it one of the finest cathedrals in Brittany. By contrast the L'Art de Cornouaille faïence shop in the corner of the square,
with its dozens of dinner plates on the wall, is definitely 'over the top'!
On the south side of the square are the Musée Départemental Breton
(see **QUIMPER-ATTRACTIONS**), the 16thC Tour de Rohan, Jardin de
l'Ancien Évêché and Rue du Parc – the boulevard beside the river
Odet. To the west is Rue du Guéodet, with sculpted gargoyles over La
Maison des Cariatides, and Rue Kéréon again (see Nos 13, 10 and 12),
leading back to the marketplace.

MUSÉE
AUTOMOBILE
DE BRETAGNE

Rue d' Antrain

BASILIQUE
ST. SAUVEUR

Rue
d' Échange

Rue St. Melaine

CATHÉDRALE
ST. PIERRE

Pl. du
Champ
Jacquet

Hoche

Rue St. Louis

Rue

PALAIS DU
PARLEMENT
BRETAGNE

Rue de la Monnaie

Rue Victor Hugo

HÔTEL
DE VILLE

Rue St. Georges

Rue

Pl. St.
Germain

Quai Duguay - Trouin

Quai Châteaubriant

Quai Lamennais

Nemours

Pl. de la
République

Quai E. Zola

La Vilaine

de

Rue Poullain - Duparc

Rue du Maréchal Joffre

Rue St. Thomas

Av.

Rue

Bd. de la Liberté

Janvier

Bd. de la Tour d' Auvergne

Rue d' Isly

MUSÉE DE
BRETAGNE
& MUSÉE DES
BEAUX-ARTS

VIEILLE VILLE *See* RENNES-WALK.

PALAIS DU PARLEMENT DU BRETAGNE Pl. du Palais.
■ 1000-1200, 1400-1800 Wed.-Mon. Guided visits 1000, 1100, 1500
& 1600. ● Free. .
*Built in 1618, this rather formal building offers visits to the Grande
Chambre, Salle des Gros Piliers, Salle des Assises and Salle des Pas
Perdus to see the paintings, Gobelin tapestries and gilded furniture.*

CATHÉDRALE ST. PIERRE Pl. de la Cathédrale.
■ 0900-1200, 1400-1700 Mon.-Sat., 0900-1200, 1700-1800 Sun.
*17thC building with 15thC Flemish wooden gilded altarpiece and
impressive organ.*

BASILIQUE ST. SAUVEUR Rue St. Sauveur.
■ 0700-1900 Mon.-Sat., 0700-1300, 1400-1900 Sun.
*Built in 1768 with a fine tower, it has an elegant pulpit and superb mod-
ern stained-glass windows.*

MUSÉE DE BRETAGNE & MUSÉE DES BEAUX-ARTS
20 quai Emile Zola. ■ 1000-1200, 1400-1800 Wed.-Mon.
● Joint ticket 30F.
*Two great museums; one for Breton local history and folklore, the other
housing a good collection of European art, ranging from Veronese to
Corot and Sisley. Note the Pont-Aven School (see A-Z) paintings, including Oranges by Gauguin, and works by the local painter J.-L. Lemordant.*

HÔTEL DE VILLE Pl. de la Mairie.
■ 0900-1200, 1400-1700 Mon.-Fri. ● Free.
*Built in 1734 with a Baroque façade and domed clock tower (Le Gros).
See the Salle des Fêtes and Panthéon.*

MUSÉE AUTOMOBILE DE BRETAGNE 40 rte de Fougères,
Cesson-Sévigné, 4 km northwest of Rennes. ■ 0900-1200, 1400-1900.
● 30F.
Collection of 70 vintage cars, fire engines and bicycles.

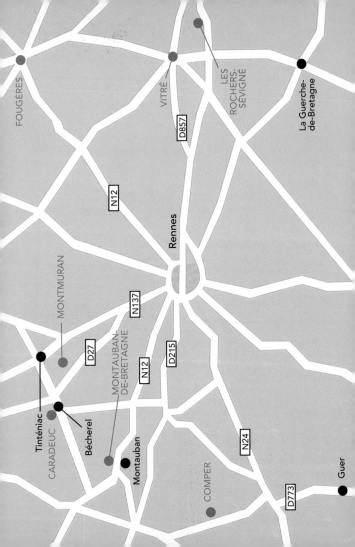

FOUGÈRES

VITRÉ

LES
ROCHERS-
SÉVIGNÉ

La Guerche-
de-Bretagne

D857

N12

Rennes

MONTMURAN

N137

D27

MONTAUBAN-
DE-BRETAGNE

N12

D215

Tinténiac

CARADEUC

Bécherel

Montauban

N24

COMPER

Guer

D773

Castles & Chateaux

FOUGÈRES 50 km northeast on the N 12.
■ 1000-1830 June-Sep., 1000-1200, 1400-1830 Mar.-May & Oct.
● 30F.
Impressive 12th-15thC feudal castle. There is a shoe museum in the Raoul tower (see RENNES-MUSEUMS).

VITRÉ 37 km east on the D 857.
■ 1000-1200, 1400-1800 July-Sep. Closed Tue. & Sat., & Sun. am.
● 17F.
11th-15thC chateau with 13 towers, drawbridge and moat. Limoges faïence and tapestries can be seen in the museum. Floodlit at night.

LES ROCHERS-SÉVIGNÉ 10 km southeast of Vitré on the D 88.
■ 1000-1200, 1330-1800 Mon.-Fri., 1400-1800 Sat. & Sun. (mid Feb.-mid Nov.). ● 20F.
15th-17thC chateau home of Marquise de Sévigné (see A-Z) who laid out the gardens and park. See RENNES-MUSEUMS.

MONTAUBAN-DE-BRETAGNE 35 km northwest on the N 12.
■ 1000-1200, 1400-1730 Wed.-Mon. (mid July-mid Sep.). ● 25F.
12thC feudal castle housing medieval weaponry and oriental sculptures.

MONTMURAN Les Iffs, 27 km northwest on the D 221.
■ 1400-1800 Easter-Oct.; Sat. & Sun., Nov.-Easter. ● 20F.
Towers flank the main 18thC building where Bertrand Du Guesclin (see A-Z) was dubbed a knight and later married.

CARADEUC Bécherel, 33 km northwest on the D 20.
■ 0900-1200, 1330-1800 April-Oct., 1400-1800 Nov.-Mar. ● Grounds only 15F.
'Le Versailles Breton'; the park has statues, summerhouses and ponds.

COMPER Concoret, 50 km west off the D 38.
■ 1000-1900 Wed.-Mon. (May-Sep.). ● 27F.
Medieval chateau with three salons. Much imagination is needed to recreate the Arthurian legends (see A-Z).

Fougères

MUSÉE DE LA CHAUSSURE

MUSÉE DE LA VILLÉON

MUSÉE DES ROCHERS-SÉVIGNÉ

La Guerche-de-Bretagne

D857

N12

Rennes

Bain-de-Bretagne

MUSÉE DE LA FAUNE

MUSÉE DE L'OUTIL ET DES MÉTIERS

N137

D27

D215

N12

Tinténiac

Bécherel

Montauban

ÉCOMUSÉE DU PAYS DE MONTFORT

MUSÉE DES ÉCOLES MILITAIRES DE ST. CYR

N24

D773

Guer

MUSÉE DE LA CHAUSSURE Pl. St. Simon, Fougères, northeast of Rennes. ■ 1000-1200, 1400-1800 Mar.-Oct. Part of the chateau guided tour. ● 30F.
The history of shoemaking and styling. See **RENNES-CASTLES & CHATEAUX**.

MUSÉE DE LA VILLÉON 51 rte Nationale, Fougères, northeast of Rennes. ■ 1400-1900 July-mid Sep. ● 17F.
A collection of Impressionists, mainly by the local Emmanuel de la Villéon.

ÉCOMUSÉE DU PAYS DE MONTFORT 2 rue du Château, Montfort-sur-Meu, west of Rennes.
■ 1000-1200, 1400-1800 Tue.-Sat. (June-Sep.). ● 17F.
Local history, folklore and costumes in the 14thC Tour du Papegaut.

MUSÉE DES ROCHERS-SÉVIGNÉ Les Rochers-Sévigné, east of Rennes. ■ 1000-1200, 1330-1800 Mon.-Fri., 1400-1800 Sat. & Sun. (mid Feb.-mid Nov.). ● 20F.
Souvenirs, portraits, letters and bric-a-brac of the authoress Marquise de Sévigné (see **A-Z**). *See* **RENNES-CASTLES & CHATEAUX**.

MUSÉE DES ÉCOLES MILITAIRES DE ST. CYR
Coëtquidan, Guer, southwest of Rennes. ■ 0900-1200, 1400-1800 Tue.-Sun., 1400-1800 Mon. ● 25F.
Military museum of three écoles – St. Cyr, Inter-Arms and Corps Technique.

MUSÉE DE L'OUTIL ET DES MÉTIERS Quai de la Dunac, Tinténiac, north of Rennes. ■ 1000-1200, 1430-1930 July-Sep. ● 17F.
Static displays of bygone crafts and their tools, including coopering, harness-making, thatching and weaving.

MUSÉE DE LA FAUNE Les Brulons, Québriac, north of Rennes.
■ 1430-1830 April-mid Oct. ● 17F.
Children will recognize many of the hundreds of stuffed animals from around the world in their 'natural' settings.

LA GROTTE

AU JARDIN
DES PLANTES

Rue d' Échange

Rue St. Melaine

L'OUVRÉE

Pl. du
Champ
Jacquet

Rue St. Louis

LE ROCHER
DE CANCALE

Hoche

Rue

Rue de la Monnaie

Rue Victor Hugo

DU PALAIS

L'ESCU DE
RUNFAO

Rue St. Georges

Pl. St.
Germain

Quai Duguay - Trouin

Quai Lamennais

Quai Châteaubriant

Pl. de la
République

Quai E. Zola

La Vilaine

Nemours

Rue Poullain - Duparc

de

Rue

Rue du Maréchal Joffre

Rue St. Thomas

Av.

MARC ANGELLE

Bd. de la Liberté

Janvier

CHOUIN

Rue d' Isly

LE GALOPIN-
GOURMET

Bd. de la Tour d' Auvergne

Restaurants

L'OUVRÉE Escale Plaisir, 18 pl. des Lices.
■ 1200-1400 Sun.-Fri., 1945-2130 Tue.-Fri. & Sun. ● Expensive.
Restaurant in a half-timbered 17thC house, noted for its lobster dishes.

MARC ANGELLE 23 rue du Maréchal Joffre.
■ 1200-1400, 1930-2200 Tue.-Sun. ● Expensive.
In a town house with an elegant courtyard garden. Try the pigeon.

L'ESCU DE RUNFAO 11 rue du Chapitre.
■ 1200-1400, 1930-2130 Mon.-Fri., 1930-2115 Sat. ● Expensive.
Restaurant in a beautiful 17thC house offering typical Breton cuisine.

CHOUIN 12 rue d'Isly.
■ 1200-1430, 1745-2130 Tue.-Sat. Closed Aug. ● Moderate.
The *restaurant for seafood in Rennes; enter through its own fish shop.*

LE GALOPIN-GOURMET 21 av. Janvier. ■ 1200-1400, 2000-2130
Mon.-Fri., 2000-2130 Sat. Closed mid July-mid Aug. ● Moderate.
Popular with tourists; good-value prix fixe menu and seafood dishes.

DU PALAIS 7 pl. du Palais.
■ 1200-1400 Tue.-Sun., 1930-2300 Tue.-Sat. Closed Aug. ● Moderate.
Smart restaurant next to parliament buildings serving nouvelle cuisine.

LE ROCHER DE CANCALE 10 rue St. Michel.
■ 1200-1415, 1930-2130 Mon.-Fri. ● Moderate.
Try le pot au feu de la mer aioli *(seafood casserole) in this rustic Breton restaurant.*

AU JARDIN DES PLANTES 32 rue St. Melaine.
■ 1200-1400, 1915-2145 Mon.-Sat. Closed Aug. ● Inexpensive.
In a medieval half-timbered house. Try the steak au poivre.

LA GROTTE 34-36 rue St. Malo.
■ 1200-1400, 2000-2130 Sun.-Fri., 2000-2130 Tue.-Sat. ● Inexpensive.
Serves delicious cassoulet au confit de canard *(duck casserole).*

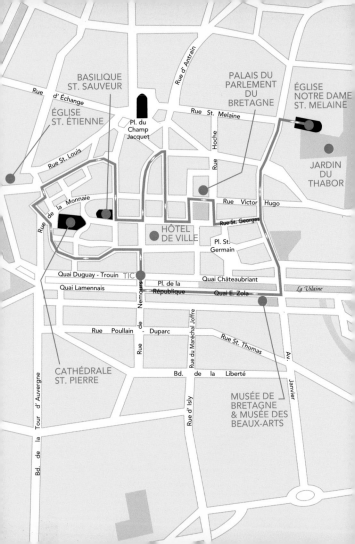

BASILIQUE
ST. SAUVEUR

PALAIS DU
PARLEMENT
DU
BRETAGNE

ÉGLISE
NOTRE DAME
ST. MELAINE

ÉGLISE
ST. ÉTIENNE

Rue d' Échange

Rue d' Antrain

Rue St. Melaine

Pl. du
Champ
Jacquet

Hoche

JARDIN
DU
THABOR

Rue St. Louis

Rue de la Monnaie

Rue Victor Hugo

Rue St. Georges

HÔTEL
DE VILLE

Pl. St.
Germain

Rue de la Monnaie

Quai Duguay - Trouin

Quai Châteaubriant

La Vilaine

Quai Lamennais

Pl. de la
République

Quai E. Zola

Nemours

Rue Poullain

Duparc

Rue St. Thomas

Rue de

Rue du Maréchal Joffre

Av.

CATHÉDRALE
ST. PIERRE

Bd. de la Liberté

Janvier

Rue d' Isly

Bd. de la Tour d' Auvergne

TIC

MUSÉE DE
BRETAGNE
& MUSÉE DES
BEAUX-ARTS

Walk

Duration: 2-3 hr.

Although a tragic fire in 1720 destroyed much of the centre of the town, the Vieille Ville is interesting and well worth a visit. The cobbled streets are lined with half-timbered houses and are mainly pedestrianized. Start at the tourist office on Pont de Nemours and head north on Rue de Rohan, then first left into Rue Beaumanoir and Pl. du Calvaire past the Hôtel de Blossac, École St. Yves and the rather jaded Chapelle St. Yves (the patron saint of lawyers and beggars). On the corner of Rue du Griffon is a tall 15thC house, now the home of the Ministry of the Environment. The Cathédrale St. Pierre (see **RENNES-ATTRACTIONS**) proudly stands with two huge five-level spires in Pl. de la Cathédrale. Its ancestry is complicated but mainly 17th-19thC, with a notable 15thC Flemish reredos (screen) in the 5th chapel on the right. There is also a rich ensemble of statues and paintings. Two hundred metres on the left in a large courtyard, near the huge covered market, is the Porte Mordelaise (1440), the only surviving medieval town gate. Continue past the marketplace in Pl. des Lices, with the Église St. Étienne on the left bordering the canal. Medieval jousts were once held here and several tall half-timbered houses (now housing pubs and doctors) overlooked the tournament courts. Next, go through Pl. St. Michel, turn right along Rue Rallier du Baty and cross Rue de la Monnaie/Rue de Toulouse past the Pub Victoria to the Basilique St. Sauveur (see **RENNES-ATTRACTIONS**) in Rue St. Sauveur. Although mainly 18thC, the church contains an interesting small chapel, Notre Dame des Miracles, commemorating the town's escape in 1357 from the marauding English troops. Go east on Rue Du Guesclin and first left past the enticing Countess de Barry *chocolaterie* in Rue Châteaurenault into Pl. du Champ Jacquet, where there are five tall half-timbered houses. Keep half right for 100 m, then turn sharp right into Rue le Bastard (named after a 19thC mayor of Rennes) and walk into the huge Pl. de la Mairie. On the left is the theatre and Brasserie Piccadilly; on the right is the Hôtel de Ville (see **RENNES-ATTRACTIONS**), built 1734-43 with a huge clock, a chapel, 17thC Brussels tapestries and a memorial hall. At the south end of the square turn left into Rue Coetquen and left again along Rue Edith Cawell (the World War I English heroine), past Gants Granet (under the hanging glove sign) into the square-gardened Pl. du Palais to

see the Palais du Parlement du Bretagne (see **RENNES-ATTRACTIONS**). This is one of Rennes' major attractions. Note the large sundial on the centre-front of the building. In the right-hand corner of the square is Cadeaux des Bretons, an excellent place to buy faïences, tablecloths, rings and bracelets, Breton dolls, lace and *coiffes* (headdresses). Keep south and at the corner of the square follow Rue St. Georges which has museums, half-timbered houses, creperies, restaurants, antique shops, and the Hôtel de Moussaye at No. 3, inside which are Le Skipper café, La Pause bar (with Celtic bagpiper sign) and the restaurant La Cotriade. Turn left on Rue Gambetta past the *piscine municipale*, some gardens and the Hôtel de Préfecture in Rue Général Guillaudot (a World War II resistance hero) to the Église Notre Dame de St. Melaine (0830-1900). This mixture of 11th, 14th and 17thC architecture was once a Benedictine abbey. At the back is a 17thC cloister with galleries and a well. The delightful 11 hectare Jardin du Thabor surrounds the church. Here there are benches, wide paths, pools and trees – an ideal spot to enjoy a picnic. Retrace your footsteps back along Rue Gambetta past the large 17thC Palais St. Georges, a Benedictine abbey which is now a bureaucratic centre with formal gardens. Cross Pl. Pasteur and go over the river Vilaine to see Rennes' two great museums at 20 quai Emile Zola – the Musée de Bretagne and Musée des Beaux-Arts (see **RENNES-ATTRACTIONS**). You are now just a few minutes' walk to the left from the tourist office.

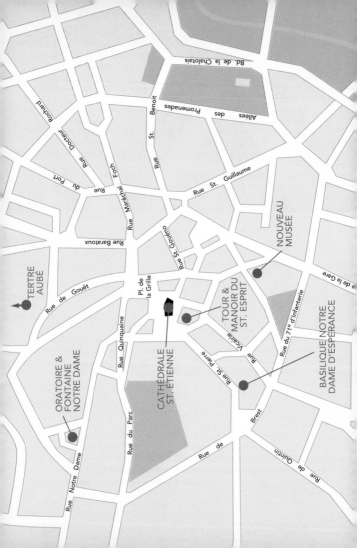

VIEILLE VILLE

There are a number of 15th-16thC houses in Rue de Gouët (Nos 6, 16, 22); Rue Fardel (Nos 15, 17, 19, 27, 29, 31, 32, 34); and Rue Quinquaine (No 9). In Pl. au Lin look out for Maison le Ribault, built in 1481. Pl. Louis-Guilloux has been renovated. Town hôtels (mansions) include the Manoir de St. Esprit, the bishop's palace, Hôtel des Ducs de Bretagne (1572), Hôtel de Rohan and Manoir de Bellescize.

CATHÉDRALE ST. ÉTIENNE Pl. Général de Gaulle.

■ 0800-1900. Closed Sun. pm.
Massive fortified 12th-13thC cathedral, restored in the 19thC and featuring two towers, a 15thC chapel, 13thC porch and tomb, and the bones and crosier of St. Guillaume. During the Revolution the cathedral became a stables, which saved it from destruction.

NOUVEAU MUSÉE Rue des Lycéens-Martyrs.

■ 0930-1145, 1330-1745 Tue.-Sun. ● 18F.
History of the Côte du Nord and Côte d'Armor.

BASILIQUE NOTRE DAME D'ESPÉRANCE Pl. St. Pierre.

■ 0800-1200, 1400-1900. Closed Sun. pm.
Still a place of pilgrimage (last Sun. in May). Note the bishop's chair and 19thC stained-glass window.

ORATOIRE & FONTAINE NOTRE DAME

Rue Notre Dame/Rue Ruffelet.
Known as Sources Orel, the Welsh monk-saint Brieuc lived here in AD 580. Note the 15thC porch and tombs of two early bishops – Fallières and Morelle.

TOUR & MANOIR DU ST. ESPRIT Pl. Général de Gaulle.

The 15thC préfecture partly conceals Renaissance buildings with an octagonal pepperpot tower.

TERTRE AUBÉ 1 km north of the cathedral.

Fine views of the Gouët valley, the port of Légué and bay of St. Brieuc.

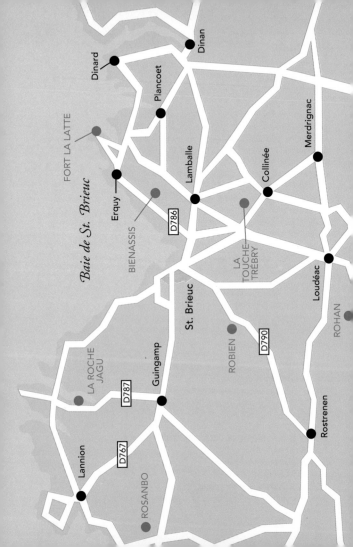

Dinan

Dinard

Plancoet

FORT LA LATTE

Merdrignac

Lamballe

Collinée

Erquy

BIENASSIS

D786

Baie de St. Brieuc

LA TOUCHE TRÉBRY

Loudéac

St. Brieuc

ROHAN

LA ROCHE JAGU

Guingamp

ROBIEN

D790

D787

Lannion

D767

Rostrenen

ROSANBO

Castles & Chateaux

BIENASSIS Erquy, 25 km northeast off the D 786.
■ 1030-1230, 1430-1830 Mon.-Sat., 1430-1830 Sun. (June-mid Sep.).
● 23F.
*Fortified 15th-17thC castle with moats, guardrooms, towers, turrets,
dining room, great salon and gardens. See DINAN-EXCURSION.*

FORT LA LATTE Cap Fréhel, 45 km northeast off the D 16a.
■ 1000-1230, 1400-1830 June-mid Sep. ● 23F.
*Overlooking the sea, this feudal castle has restored drawbridges, ram-
parts, dungeons and a cannonball foundry. See DINAN-EXCURSION.*

LA TOUCHE TRÉBRY Moncontour, 30 km southeast off the D 25.
■ 1400-1800 Mon.-Sat. (July & Aug.). ● 18F.
*Late-medieval castle beside a 5 hectare lake. See the fireplaces,
tapestries and furnishings, and also note the domed towers, jousting
pitch and the well in the courtyard.*

ROBIEN Quintin, 18 km southwest on the D 790.
■ 1000-1230, 1400-1830 Mon.-Sat. (Mar.-Aug.). ● Free.
*Visit the park, 18thC chateau and small museum. There is an ideal
picnic spot by the river Gouët and a separate ruined 17thC castle.*

ROHAN Pontivy, 65 km south on the D 768.
■ 1000-1230, 1400-1800 Tue.-Sun. ● 35F summer, 10F winter.
*Exhibitions and concerts are held in midsummer in this 15thC fortress.
See the duke's chamber and chapel.*

LA ROCHE JAGU Ploezal, 50 km northwest off the D 787.
■ 1000-1300, 1400-1900 April-mid Sep.; Sun. (mid Sep.-Mar.). ● 25F.
15thC castle with 19 Gothic fireplaces, on slopes above the river Trieux.

ROSANBO Lanvellec, 60 km west off the D 32.
■ 1000-1200, 1400-1800 July & Aug.; Sat. & Sun. (April-June & Sep.).
● 23F.
*14th-17thC chateau with fine living rooms, furnishings, tapestries, library
and restaurant. The Louis XIII and XIV furniture is highly praised.*

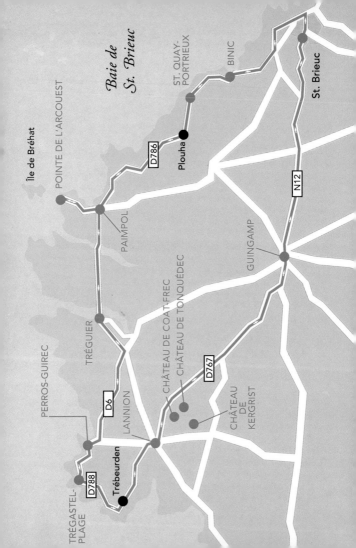

Baie de
St. Brieuc

Île de Bréhat

POINTE DE L'ARCOUEST

ST. QUAY-PORTRIEUX

BINIC

St. Brieuc

D786

Plouha

N12

PAIMPOL

GUINGAMP

PERROS-GUIREC

TRÉGUIER

CHÂTEAU DE COAT-FREC

CHÂTEAU DE TONQUÉDEC

D6

LANNION

D767

CHÂTEAU DE KERGRIST

TRÉGASTEL-PLAGE

D788

Trébeurden

A one-day excursion to Paimpol, Tréguier, Lannion and Guingamp.

Take Av. Corneille east to join the N 12, then cross the viaduct over the river Gouët. After 8 km join the D 786 to Binic (pop: 2600), a small resort and fishing port with a Newfoundland fishing museum (1000-1200, 1400-1830 mid June-mid Sep.; 17F). Continue through Étables-sur-Mer.

24 km – St. Quay-Portrieux (pop: 3400) is a major resort which has five beaches, a sea-water *piscine* on the sands and a casino. Summer regattas, and tennis, golf and riding tournaments, plus discos at night make it almost as lively as Dinard. The hotel-restaurants Ker Moor and Le Gerbot d'Avoine are recommended. Follow the D 786 inland to Plouha (pop: 4300) and north for 15 km past the decaying Abbaye de Beauport.

49 km – Paimpol. Pop: 8400. A modern fishing port with little bistros and bars along the quayside. Oysters are an important industry here. The Musée de la Mer (1000-1200, 1400-1830 mid June-mid Sep.; 20F) is on Quai Loti (Pierre Loti, the novelist, wrote about Paimpol). The local pirate Pierre Kersaux built the Hôtel-Restaurant Repaire de Kerroc'h, 29 quai Morand, in 1793. Vedettes leave to visit the Île de Bréhat (see **Islands**), 3 km offshore from the Pointe de l'Arcouest which is reached by the D 789 to the north. There are delightful views from both the island and the headland. Follow the D 786 westwards from Paimpol.

76 km – Tréguier (pop: 3400) is across the wide estuary of the tidal river Trieux. Visit the majestic three-towered 13th-15thC cathedral of St. Tugdual. Note the three large stained-glass windows commemorating World War I. The 15thC cloister and *trésor* can be visited (17F). St. Yves is the saint who stood for justice in the 13thC and his 'renovated' tomb can be seen. Four times an hour, the five church bells peel the saint's own canticle. The Musée Ernest Rénan (1000-1200, 1400-1800 Thu.-Mon., Easter-Sep.; 23F), where the historian lived and worked, is 200 m east of the cathedral in a 16thC house. Around the town flow two rivers, the Gindy and Jaudy. The little marina is on the latter. Keep on the D 786 for 6 km, then turn off on the D 6 for 15 km to Perros-Guirec (pop: 7500) which is the largest resort on the north coast, with two

Loguivy, Paimpol

beaches, a marina and a fishing port. Trestraou Plage is popular and has a casino, several hotels and restaurants and a *centre de thalassothérapie* (sea-water therapy). Vedette excursions leave here for Les Sept Îles. Continue for 3 km to the west. Trégastel-Plage (pop: 2000) is famous for its extraordinary rocks, many of which are individually named. There are three beaches, the Aquarium de la Côte de Granit Rose (1030-1830 June-mid Sep., 1400-1830 Mon.-Fri., mid Sep.-May; 23F) with a fine collection of Channel and tropical fish, and seven hotels. Take the D 788 via Trébeurden.

105 km – Lannion. Pop: 17,000. Bisected by the river Léguer this inland port has the hill-top 12th-15thC Église de Brélévénez, 16th-17thC Église de St. Jean-du-Baly and a score of medieval houses in Rue des Chapeliers, Pl. du Général Leclerc and Rue Cie-Roger-Barbé. To the southeast between the D 11 and D 767 are three notable chateaux: Tonquédec, dating from the 13th-15thC with towers and a keep (1000-1200, 1400-1800 July & Aug.; 15F); Coat-Frec,

a handsome 16thC pile in need of repairs (free); and Kergrist, a 14th-15thC chateau set in French- and English-style landscaped gardens (1400-1800 Wed.-Mon., July-mid Sep., Sat. & Sun, May & June; 23F).

137 km – Guingamp. Pop: 9500. The river Trieux runs through this inland agricultural town with its 14thC basilica, Notre Dame de Bon Secours. On the first weekend in July there is the great pardon (see **A-Z**) to see the Black Virgin in a side chapel of the church. There are some medieval houses in Pl. du Centre, a Hôtel de Ville of 1699 and a few ramparts, but Richelieu had the castle destroyed. Two inexpensive hotels are the D'Armor and L'Escale, and restaurants to try include Relais du Roy, 42 pl. du Centre, and Chaumière, 42 rue de la Trinitée. The N 12 continues eastwards back to St. Brieuc.

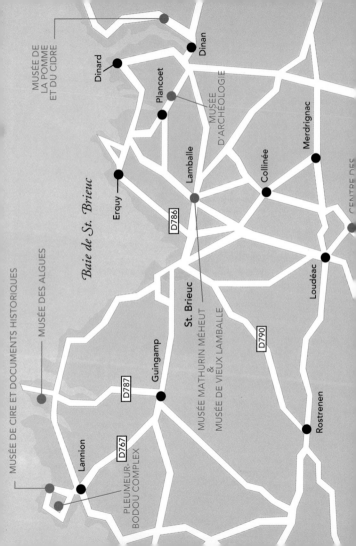

MUSÉE DE LA POMME ET DU CIDRE

Dinan

Dinard

Plancoet

MUSÉE D'ARCHÉOLOGIE

Merdrignac

Lamballe

Collinée

Erquy

Baie de St. Brieuc

D786

St. Brieuc

Loudéac

CENTRE DES

MUSÉE DES ALGUES

MUSÉE DE CIRE ET DOCUMENTS HISTORIQUES

Guingamp

MUSÉE MATHURIN MÉHEUT & MUSÉE DE VIEUX LAMBALLE

D790

D787

Rostrenen

Lannion

D767

PLEUMEUR-BODOU COMPLEX

MUSÉE D'ARCHÉOLOGIE
Corseul, east of St. Brieuc. ■ 1000-1200, 1400-1700 Mon.-Sat. (July & Aug.); 1000-1200 Sep.-June. ● 17F.
Prehistoric and Gallo-Roman finds in the town hall, including artefacts of the Coriosolite tribe. Try to visit the garden of antiquities next door.

CENTRE DES MÉTIERS DE BRETAGNE
La Chèze, south of St. Brieuc. ■ 1400-1800 Tue.-Sun. (June-mid Sep.). ● 17F.
The crafts of the saddler, cartwright, clog-maker, slate-cutter, joiner and blacksmith are on view.

MUSÉE MATHURIN MÉHEUT & MUSÉE DE VIEUX LAMBALLE
Pl. du Martray, Lamballe, east of St. Brieuc. ■ 1000-1200, 1430-1830 Mon.-Sat. (June-Sep.). ● Joint ticket 16F.
On the 1st floor are sketches and watercolours by the painter (1882-1955) of traditional Brittany, while the ground floor houses costumes, lace, headdresses, clay models, statues, prehistoric weapons and tools.
See **DINAN-EXCURSION**.

MUSÉE DE CIRE ET DOCUMENTS HISTORIQUES
Port le Liaken, Perros-Guirec, north of Lannion. ■ 0930-1230, 1400-1930 July & Aug., 1430-1900 Wed., Sat. & Sun. (Sep.-June). ● 20F.
The French Revolution in wax figures, and the history of the Trégor area.

MUSÉE DES ALGUES
Pleubian, northwest of St. Brieuc. ■ 1400-1630 Tue. & Thu. (July & Aug.). ● Free.
Seaweed research establishment. Seaweed-gathering is still a local job and over 70 varieties have been documented.

MUSÉE DE LA POMME ET DU CIDRE
Pleudihen-sur-Rance, northeast of Dinan. ■ 1000-1200, 1400-1800 Easter-Nov. ● Free.
From apples to cider, with exhibitions, films and cider-tasting.

PLEUMEUR-BODOU COMPLEX
6 km northwest of Lannion. ■ July & Aug. Ask at tourist offices for details.
Bird sanctuary, nature walks, planetarium, Radome Telecom centre and Gallic village. Ideal for a family visit.

Restaurants

L'AMADEUS 22 rue de Gouët.
■ 1200-1400 Tue.-Sun., 1930-2130 Mon.-Sat. (July-Aug.). ● Moderate.
Trendy restaurant in a half-timbered house with Mozart himself gazing out of the window. The salmon with mustard is recommended.

HÔTEL-RESTAURANT DU GUESCLIN 2 pl. Du Guesclin.
■ 1100-2300. ● Moderate.
A large brasserie-restaurant with a terrace. Try the sole soufflé.

LE MADURE 14 rue Quinquaine.
■ 1200-1400, 1900-2300 Mon.-Fri., 1900-2300 Sat. ● Moderate.
Grills over a wood fire. Do not be deterred by the dowdy façade.

HÔTEL-RESTAURANT LE CHAMP DE MARS Pl. du Champ de Mars. ■ 1200-1400 Tue.-Sat., 1800-2145 Mon.-Sat. ● Moderate.
Try moules au cidre *in Art Deco surroundings overlooking a large square.*

LE BISTROT DU PORT 15 rue Trois-Frères-Le-Goff.
■ 1200-1400, 1900-2330 Thu.-Tue. ● Moderate.
The prix fixe menus include apéritif, wine and coffee.

LE CHAUDRON 19 rue Fardel. ■ 1200-1345, 1930-2130 Mon., Tue. & Thu.-Sat., 1930-2130 Wed. ● Moderate.
In a 17thC half-timbered town house. Try the symphonie de la mer.

LA GRILLE 6 rue Trois-Frères-Le-Goff.
■ 1200-1400, 1930-2200. ● Inexpensive.
Simple lace-curtained creperie-grill serving seafood dishes. Three menus.

LA JONQUIÈRE Pl. au Lin.
■ 1100-2300. ● Inexpensive.
Large, modern restaurant-glacier with three good cheap fish menus.

LE TOURNEBRIDE 10 rue Mireille-Chrisostome.
■ 1200-1345, 1900-2100 Mon.-Sat. ● Inexpensive.
Two prix fixe menus include boeuf bourguignon.

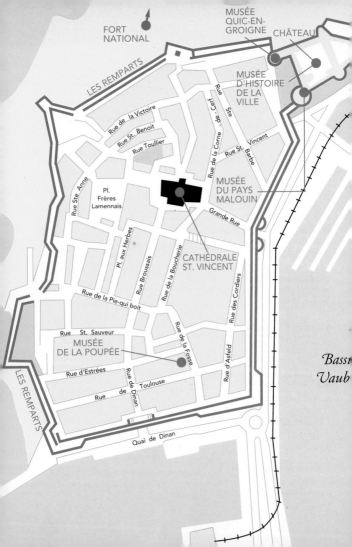

FORT
NATIONAL

MUSÉE
QUIC-EN-
GROIGNE

CHÂTEAU

LES REMPARTS

MUSÉE
D'HISTOIRE
DE LA
VILLE

Rue de la Victoire

Rue St. Benoit

Rue Toullier

Rue de la Corne - de - Cerf

Rue Ste Vincent

Rue St. Barbe

MUSÉE
DU PAYS
MALOUIN

Rue Ste Anne

Pl.
Frères
Lamennais

Grande Rue

Pl. aux Herbes

Rue Broussais

Rue de la Boucherie

CATHÉDRALE
ST. VINCENT

Rue des Cordiers

Rue de la Pie-qui boit

Rue   St. Sauveur

MUSÉE
DE LA POUPÉE

Rue de la Fosse

Rue d'Estrées

Rue de Dinan

Rue   de   Toulouse

Rue d'Asfeld

Quai de Dinan

LES REMPARTS

Bassi
Vaub

Attractions

LES REMPARTS *See* ST. MALO-WALK.

CHÂTEAU Porte St. Vincent.
Houses the Hôtel de Ville and three museums (see below). There are colourful son et lumière (see A-Z) shows during the summer.

MUSÉE D'HISTOIRE DE LA VILLE Hôtel de Ville.
■ 0900-1200, 1400-1830 Wed.-Mon. ● 22F.
Houses maps, documents and prints of the famous citizens of St. Malo: the explorer Jacques Cartier (see A-Z); Chateaubriand (see A-Z) and Lamenais, the writers; Maupertuis, the mathematician; and a couple of distinguished corsairs (see A-Z) – Duguay-Trouin and Robert Surcouf.

MUSÉE QUIC-EN-GROIGNE North tower of the château.
■ 0930-1200, 1400-1800 Wed.-Mon. (Easter-Oct.). ● 25F.
Waxwork museum showing eight centuries of St. Malo history.

MUSÉE DU PAYS MALOUIN La Générale tower of the château.
■ 0930-1200, 1400-1800 Wed.-Mon. ● 23F.
A more modern museum showing economic and geographic aspects of St. Malo, and its fishing traditions.

CATHÉDRALE ST. VINCENT Pl. Jean de Chatillon.
■ 0800-1830.
Rebuilt in original Gothic style after Aug. 1944, it has a 12thC nave, tombs (including that of Duguay-Trouin), outstanding stained-glass windows and poignant wall plaques to the fallen of World War II (see A-Z).

MUSÉE DE LA POUPÉE 13 rue de Toulouse.
■ 1000-1200, 1400-1900 July & Aug. ● 25F.
More than 300 dolls are on display.

FORT NATIONAL On an islet 300 m north of the town.
■ 1000-1200, 1400-1800 Wed.-Mon. ● 20F.
Designed by Vauban in 1689, and reached on foot at low tide. See the guard walls, courtyard and dungeons.

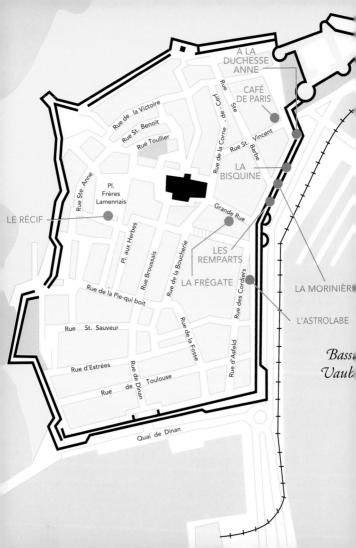

À LA
DUCHESSE
ANNE

CAFÉ
DE PARIS

Rue de la Victoire

Rue St. Benoît

Rue Toullier

Rue de la Corne - de - Cerf

Rue Ste

Rue St. Barbe

Rue St. Vincent

LA
BISQUINE

Rue Ste Anne

Pl.
Frères
Lamennais

LE RÉCIF

Grande Rue

Pl. aux Herbes

Rue Broussais

Rue de la Boucherie

LES
REMPARTS

LA FRÉGATE

Rue de la Pie-qui boît

Rue des Cordiers

LA MORINIÈR

L'ASTROLABE

Rue St. Sauveur

Rue de la Fosse

Rue d'Estrées

Rue de Dinan

Rue d'Asfeld

Rue de Toulouse

Bass
Vaul

Rue de Dinan

Quai de Dinan

Restaurants

NOTE: *All selected restaurants are within the ramparts; most are closed during the winter months.*

À LA DUCHESSE ANNE 5-7 pl. Guy la Chambre.
■ 1200-1400, 2000-2130 Thu.-Tue. Closed Dec. & Jan. ● Expensive.
Authentic 1920s ambience: serves grilled turbot and lobster dishes.

LA FRÉGATE Hôtel-Restaurant Central, 6 Grande Rue.
■ 1145-1345, 1900-2030. ● Expensive.
A smart Art Deco restaurant. The grilled red mullet in anchovy butter (barbue pochée au beurre) is recommended.

L'ASTROLABE 8 rue des Cordiers.
■ 1200-1430, 1930-2200 Tue.-Sat., 1200-1400 Sun. ● Moderate.
The blanquette de poisson (fish stew) is recommended.

LA MORINIÈRE 9 rue Jacques Cartier.
■ 1200-1400, 2000-2130 Wed.-Mon. ● Moderate.
In ramparts with paintings on the walls. Try langoustines royales grillées.

LA BISQUINE 21 rue Jacques Cartier.
■ 1200-1430, 1930-2200. Closed Thu., Oct.-May. ● Moderate.
Excellent seafood dishes in this large, rambling, old-fashioned setting.

LES REMPARTS 17 rue Jacques Cartier.
■ 1200-2300 Sat.-Thu. ● Moderate.
Huddled under the ramparts, with tables outside from which to watch the world go by. Try the saumonette à la crème d'ail (salmon and garlic).

LE RÉCIF 11 rue du Boyer.
■ 1200-1430, 1930-2200 Fri.-Wed. ● Inexpensive.
Grilled meat and fish dishes, as well as crêpes Quimperoises.

CAFÉ DE PARIS 2 pl. Guy la Chambre.
■ 1130-2130. ● Inexpensive.
Large, noisy brasserie. Grilled sardines and mackerel are recommended.

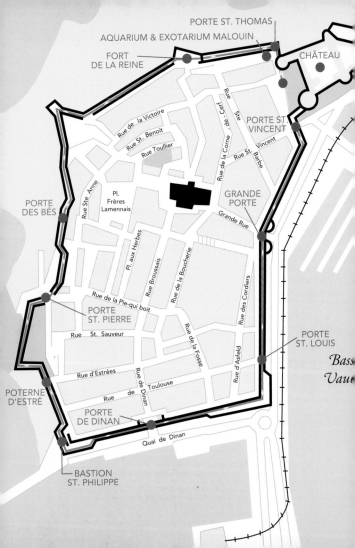

PORTE ST. THOMAS

AQUARIUM & EXOTARIUM MALOUIN

FORT
DE LA REINE

CHÂTEAU

Rue de la Corne - de - Cerf

Rue Ste - Anne

Rue de la Victoire

Rue St. Benoît

Rue Toullier

PORTE ST.
VINCENT

Rue St. Barbe

Rue St. Vincent

Rue Ste Anne

Pl.
Frères
Lamennais

PORTE
DES BÉS

GRANDE
PORTE

Grande Rue

Pl. aux Herbes

Rue Broussais

Rue de la Boucherie

Rue des Cordiers

Rue de la Pie-qui boit

PORTE
ST. PIERRE

Rue   St. Sauveur

Rue de la Fosse

PORTE
ST. LOUIS

Rue d'Estrées

Rue   de   Dinan

Rue d'Asfeld

Bass
Vaue

POTERNE
D'ESTRÉ

Rue   de   Toulouse

PORTE
DE DINAN

Quai de Dinan

BASTION
ST. PHILIPPE

Walk

Duration: 1.5-2 hr.

The rampart walk extending 2.5 km round the town affords excellent views outwards (marinas, ports, islands, beaches) and inwards over the rebuilt town, of which the cathedral and Chapelle St. Sauveur are the most notable buildings. Large photographs show the appalling damage the town suffered during two weeks in Aug. 1944 (see **World War II**). A number of staircases ascend from the cobbled streets onto the ramparts. Start at Porte St. Vincent just south of the chateau and walk south and clockwise. To the left is the port (and tourist office) and, inside, Rue Jacques Cartier which has a dozen or more seafood restaurants. The Grande Porte overlooks Pl. du Poids du Roi and Grande Rue leading to the cathedral. Another 400 m south is the Porte St. Louis and the statue of Duguay-Trouin, the great St. Malo corsair (see **A-Z**). The *gare maritime* is to the left, where ferries, vedettes and *aéro-glisseurs* (hover-craft) leave for the islands or the UK. Inside the walls are Rue de Chartres and Rue d'Orléans. The rampart walk heads 300 m west past the Porte de Dinan to the Bastion St. Philippe, and north past the Poterne d'Estré and statue of Jacques Cartier (see **A-Z**) to the Porte St. Pierre. To the southwest and west are superb views of the river Rance, the *barrage* (dam) and Dinard. At low tide there are several beaches. Next is the Porte des Bés, and a statue of Robert Surcouf with his arm aloft, perhaps in the act of boarding an English vessel. Out to sea is the Île de Grand Bé, which can be visited at low tide, with Chateaubriand's (see **A-Z**) tomb. At Passage de la Poudrière the ramparts head northeast parallel to Rue du Château Gaillard to Fort de la Reine and Poterne aux Normands, with views of Fort National (see **ST. MALO-ATTRACTIONS**). Inside the walls are the École d'Hydrographie, Chapelle St. Aaron and Maison de la Duchesse Anne (2 cour de la Houssaye). In Pl. Vauban are the Aquarium and Exotarium Malouin (0930-2300; joint ticket 36F), of which the former has an amazing collection of marine life and coral (you can walk on top of it!), while the latter specializes in everything from crocodiles to tortoises. Nearby is the great Château (see **ST. MALO-ATTRACTIONS**), of which the keep was built in 1424, the corner towers in the 15th-16thC and the bailey and chapel in the 17thC. By the Porte St. Thomas take the steps down into Pl. Chateaubriand which has several good hotel-restaurants.

St. Malo

CE MONUMENT A ETE ERIGE POUR PERPETUER
LE SOUVENIR DES HOMMES ET DES FEMMES
DE LA RESISTANCE FRANÇAISE QUI PENDANT
LA SECONDE GUERRE MONDIALE ONT LUTTE
CONTRE L'OCCUPANT NAZI, SONT TOMBES AU
CHAMP D'HONNEUR, ONT ETE FUSILLES, ONT
ETE EXTERMINES DANS LES CAMPS DE
CONCENTRATION

" PASSANT RECUEILLE-TOI ET MEDITE DEVANT CET ENCLOS
QUI CONTIENT DES CENDRES DE CES MARTYRS "

PATRIA NON
IMMEMOR

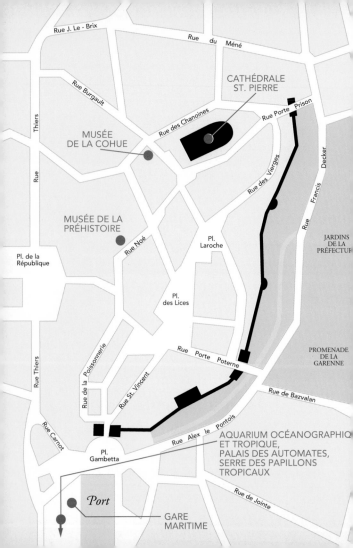

Rue J. Le - Brix

Rue du Méné

Rue Burgault

Rue des Chanoines

CATHÉDRALE
ST. PIERRE

Rue Porte Prison

Rue Thiers

MUSÉE
DE LA COHUE

Rue des Vierges

Rue Francis Decker

JARDINS
DE LA
PRÉFECTURE

MUSÉE DE LA
PRÉHISTOIRE

Rue Noé

Pl.
Laroche

Pl. de la
République

Pl.
des Lices

PROMENADE
DE LA
GARENNE

Rue Porte Poterne

Rue de la Poissonnerie

Rue de Bazvalan

Rue Thiers

Rue St. Vincent

Rue Carnot

Rue Alex le Pontois

Pl.
Gambetta

AQUARIUM OCÉANOGRAPHIQUE
ET TROPIQUE,
PALAIS DES AUTOMATES,
SERRE DES PAPILLONS
TROPICAUX

Rue de Jointe

Port

GARE
MARITIME

Attractions

VIEILLE VILLE *See* VANNES-WALK.

GARE MARITIME Promenade de la Rabine.
Hundreds of yachts berth in the marina. Vedettes Vertes visit the 12,000 hectare Golfe du Morbihan with its 365 islands.

CATHÉDRALE ST. PIERRE Pl. St. Pierre.
■ 0800-1800. Closed Sun. pm. ● Treasury June-Sep. 6F.
The cathedral features a 13th-19thC Romanesque belfry, strong buttresses, gargoyles, statues, chapels and stained-glass windows.

MUSÉE DE LA COHUE 9-15 pl. St. Pierre/rue des Halles. Contains the Musée des Beaux-Arts and Musée du Golfe et de la Mer.
■ 1000-1200, 1400-1800 mid June-mid Sep.; Wed.-Sat. & Mon., mid Sep.-mid June. ● Joint ticket 15F.
In the former museum you can see the Delacroix Crucifixion *and Pont-Aven School (see* **A-Z**) *paintings. The latter is Yves Duhamel's museum showing the fishing life and traditions of the Golfe du Morbihan.*

MUSÉE DE LA PRÉHISTOIRE Chateau Gaillard, 2 rue Noé.
■ 1400-1800 Mon.-Fri. ● 20F.
Exhibits of archaeology and 17thC furniture in a 15thC manor house. Look out for the 17thC cabinet de travail with 66 wooden panels.

AQUARIUM OCÉANOGRAPHIQUE ET TROPIQUE Parc du Golfe. ■ 0900-1900 July & Aug., 0900-1200, 1330-1830 Sep.-June.
● 45F.
50 pools house fish and coral from around the world.

PALAIS DES AUTOMATES Parc du Golfe. ■ 1000-1200, 1400-1830 April-June, 1000-1900 July & Aug., 1400-1830 Sep.-Mar. ● 30F.
A strange collection of automatic dolls and musical instruments.

SERRE DES PAPILLONS TROPICAUX Parc du Golfe.
■ 1000-1900 May-Oct. ● 30F.
500 different butterflies fly freely in luxuriant equatorial vegetation.

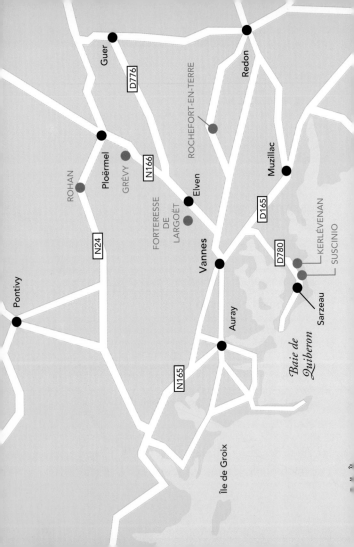

Castles & Chateaux

ROCHEFORT-EN-TERRE 36 km east on the D 777.
■ 1030-1200, 1400-1800 June-Sep.; Sat. & Sun. (April & May). ● 25F.
Recently well restored by an American family, with a small folklore museum in the gardens. Note the salons, pictures, tapestries, Quimper porcelain and hunting pavilion. See **VANNES-EXCURSION 1**.

KERLÉVENAN Sarzeau, 22 km south on the D 780.
■ 1400-1800 July-mid Sep. ● Free but tel: 97264110 to view.
17thC Italianate white-stone castle with chapel, temple of love and Chinese pavilion. See **VANNES-EXCURSION 1**.

SUSCINIO Sarzeau, 27 km south on the D 198.
■ 0930-1200, 1400-1900 April-Sep.; Tue., Sat. & Sun. (Oct.-Mar.).
● 25F.
13th-16thC fortress near the Atlantic. Hosts a festival 1st two weeks in Aug. Very impressive but windswept. See **VANNES-EXCURSION 1**.

FORTERESSE DE LARGOËT Elven, 14 km northeast off the N 166. ■ 0800-1200, 1400-1730 mid Jan.-mid Nov. ● 18F.
14thC feudal castle with an octagonal keep and drawbridge. Son et lumière (see **A-Z***) shows in July & Aug., usually on Arthurian themes. See* **VANNES-EXCURSION 3**.

ROHAN Josselin, 48 km northeast on the D 4.
■ 1000-1200, 1400-1800 July & Aug., 1400-1800 Mar.-June & Sep.
● 30F.
Magnificent 16thC fortress-chateau beside the river Oust with three large towers, ramparts and a separate doll museum (see **VANNES-MUSEUMS***). See* **VANNES-EXCURSION 3**.

GRÉVY La Chapelle-Caro, 40 km northeast on the N 166.
■ 1000-1200, 1400-1800 July-mid Sep.; 1400-1800 Wed., Sat. & Sun. (April, May & mid Sep.-Nov.). ● 35F.
The philosopher Descartes lived in this handsome Loire-style chateau whose salons house a collection of 18thC costumes. See **VANNES-EXCURSION 3**.

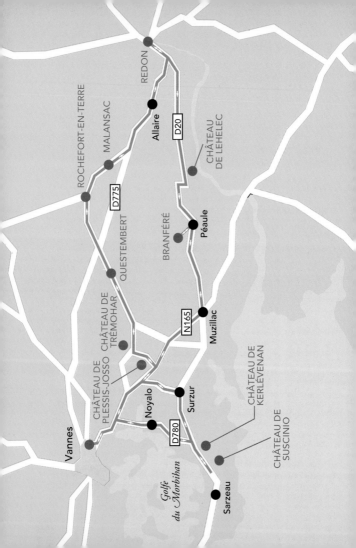

REDON

ROCHEFORT-EN-TERRE

MALANSAC

Allaire

D20

CHÂTEAU DE LEHELEC

D775

QUESTEMBERT

BRANFÉRÉ

Péaule

N165

Muzillac

CHÂTEAU DE TRÉMOHAR

CHÂTEAU DE PLESSIS-JOSSO

CHÂTEAU DE KERLÉVENAN

Noyalo

Surzur

Vannes

D780

CHÂTEAU DE SUSCINIO

Sarzeau

Golfe du Morbihan

Excursion 1

A one-day excursion to Rochefort-en-Terre and Redon.

Take the D 779 east out of Vannes, briefly join the N 165 and then take the D 780 south past Noyalo to two chateaux on the Rhuys peninsula, which forms the eastern arm of the Golfe du Morbihan. Before you reach Sarzeau there is the Château de Kerlévenan (see **VANNES-CASTLES & CHATEAUX**) and 4 km to the south down a minor road is the Château de Suscinio (see **VANNES-CASTLES & CHATEAUX**) overlooking the Atlantic. Return to the D 780 and fork right and east for 8 km into Surzur on the D 20. Follow the D 183 for 4 km to two more chateaux – Plessis-Josso (1400-1900 July & Aug.; 23F), a mainly 15thC chateau with a Louis XVIII pavilion, and Trémohar (closed to the public). Follow the D 7 east to Questembert, with its medieval market hall. Keep on the D 777.

76 km – Rochefort-en-Terre, with its chateau (see **VANNES-CASTLES & CHATEAUX**), 12th-15thC church and old houses, must rank as one of the prettiest villages in Brittany. On a hill overlooking the Gueuzon and Arz rivers, it gets very crowded in summer. The many artisans practise glass-blowing, pottery and woodworking. The honey is excellent; possibly the bees like the flowers for which the village is noted. Drive southeast for 2.5 km on the D 21 to Malansac, where there is a Parc de Préhistoire (1000-2000 June-Sep.; 30F). Continue on the D 313 for 5.5 km and east on the D 775 to Allaire, then along a wooded road.

101 km – Redon. Pop: 10,000. Although the town contains some medieval houses in Grande Rue, Rue Jean d'Arc and Rue d'Enfer, the city fathers could have tried harder to preserve more of medieval Redon. However, it can still boast the abbey church of St. Sauveur with its separate bell tower, the small marina from where there are vedette excursions, and a handsome *mairie* and theatre. The restaurant La Bugue in Pl. de Parlement is recommended. From Redon take the D 20. After 18 km, just past Béganne, is the Château de Lehelec (1400-1900 Wed.-Mon., July & Aug.; 23F), a majestic pink-granite manor house. Continue for 9 km to Péaule, then turn left for Branféré (0900-1200, 1400-1830 mid April-mid Nov.). A 45F ticket lets you see the original 14thC Templar chateau, 50 hectares of parkland, lakes and a zoo containing different exotic animals and birds in natural settings. Go back to Le Guerno on the D 139, the D 20 to Muzillac and on to Vannes.

Excursion 2

A one-day excursion to Carnac, Quiberon and Belle-Île.

Equipped with anoraks (for the sea-crossing from Quiberon to Belle-Île), set off as early as you can as this will be a long day! Take the N 165 signposted to Auray. After 18 km take the D 28 and D 781 to Locmariaquer (pop: 1250) which has four superb dolmens and menhirs, and views of the vast Golfe du Morbihan. Vedettes Vertes call at the little port. Keep west on the D 781 across the river Crac'h with superb views. Immediately after, head inland to see the astonishing *alignements* (see **Carnac**), row upon row of huge standing stones among the bracken, fern and pine woods. Erected by a seafaring but nomadic early-Neolithic tribe several thousand years ago, their presence inspires awe and amazement. Whatever their purpose – perhaps religious or astronomical – the physical achievement was incredible. North of Carnac there are altogether some 4000 boulders.

44 km – Carnac has a fashionable *plage* and marina, as well as the church of St. Cornely which hosts a pardon (see **A-Z**) in Sep., and two Benedictine abbeys 3 km northwest (Ste Anne and St. Michel). Take the D 768 south past the Musée le Galion (0900-1800 July & Aug., 0900-1200, 1400-1800 April-June; 17F), displaying seashells, in Plouharnel, then 15 km via St. Pierre-Quiberon with its beaches, port and a small *alignement*.

62 km – Quiberon (pop: 5000) has beaches, a casino and small airport, a *thalassothérapie* (sea-water therapy) resort and the busy Port Maria. The vedettes take cars and several hundred passengers to Belle-Île (see **Islands**), and the exhilarating sea voyage lasts 45 min (80F return). Arrival is at Le Palais, which has small outer and inner harbours and is dominated by the huge fortress built by Vauban on the north side. Local bus tours are frequent (60F for half-day tour). Restaurants include L'Odyssée, Le Goeland (with evening jazz) and Les Niniches. On returning to Quiberon take the picturesque Côte Sauvage route, the D 186 on the western side of the isthmus, past headlands, low-tide beaches, occasional menhirs and the Fort de Ponthièvre, then back onto the D 768. Continue northeast. The really energetic traveller can visit Auray (see **A-Z**) and Ste Anne d'Auray (see **A-Z**), both of which are well worth a detour. It is then 18 km east to Vannes.

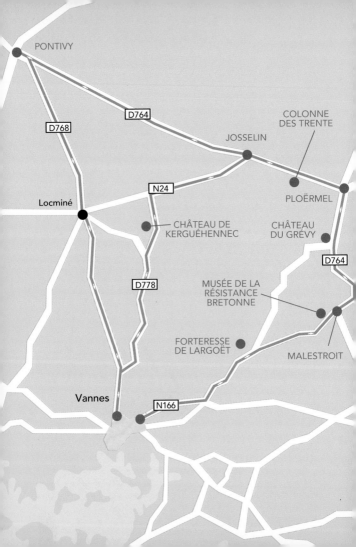

A one-day excursion to Ploërmel and Josselin.

Leave Vannes by the N 165 and N 166. About 3 km before Elven there is a minor road on the left, signed for Forteresse de Largoët (see **VANNES-CASTLES & CHATEAUX**). Take the N 166 and D 776 to the Musée de la Résistance Bretonne (see **VANNES-MUSEUMS**) at St. Marcel.

50 km – Malestroit (pop: 2500), beside the Oust canal, is worth a stop to see the medieval squares round the 12th-16thC church of St. Gilles, with its double nave, stained-glass windows and interesting carvings of saints on the south doorway. Cross the canal and take the D 764 north-west for 10 km to see the 14thC pepperpot-turreted Château du Grévy (see **VANNES-CASTLES & CHATEAUX**). Take the N 166 north for 8 km.

66 km – Ploërmel (pop: 7250) calls itself 'Cité des Ducs de Bretagne'. Founded by the 6thC St. Armel, Ploërmel was occupied by the English during the Hundred Years' War. The 16thC church of St. Armel has a fine north portal, 20 stained-glass windows (including a Tree of Jesse of 1552), tombs, a wooden barrel-shaped roof and gargoyles galore. A dozen medieval houses, some ramparts, an astronomical clock and the Musée La Mennais (1000-1200, 1400-1800 April-mid Sep.; 15F) are worth a look. Northwest is the Lac de Ploërmel, a boating, fishing and camping paradise, and northeast is the Pays des Légendes, the setting for the Arthurian legends (see **A-Z**) in and around the Forêt de Paimpont. Keep west on the N 24 past the Colonne des Trente, a pyramid commemorating the strange 60-man 'duel' in 1351 in which the French équipe beat the English-German-Breton team.

78 km – Josselin. Pop: 2750. The marvellous Château de Rohan (see **VANNES-CASTLES & CHATEAUX**) ranks among the best in Brittany. The 11thC basilica of Notre Dame, 17thC pilgrimage fountain, Musée des Poupées (see **VANNES-MUSEUMS**) and medieval houses all make Josselin a lovely little town to visit. From Josselin there are two alternatives:
Either: Go northwest for 32 km on the D 764 to Pontivy (see **A-Z**).
Or: Take the N 24 (signed Locminé) but after 12 km follow the D 11 to Château de Kerguéhennec (1000-1900 July & Aug.; Sat. & Sun., April-June, Sep. & Oct.; 25F). This 18thC Loire-style chateau hosts up to 20 exhibitions simultaneously, including 16 in the woodlands. The D 778 passes various menhirs and joins the D 767 back to Vannes.

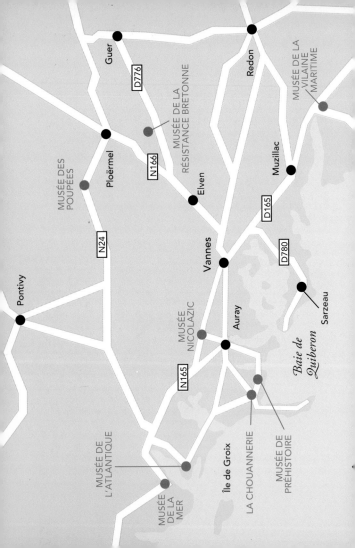

Guer

D776

MUSÉE DE LA RÉSISTANCE BRETONNE

Redon

MUSÉE DE LA VILAINE MARITIME

Ploërmel

MUSÉE DES POUPÉES

N166

Muzillac

Elven

D165

N24

Vannes

D780

Pontivy

Sarzeau

MUSÉE NICOLAZIC

Auray

Baie de Quiberon

N165

Île de Groix

LA CHOUANNERIE

MUSÉE DE PRÉHISTOIRE

MUSÉE DE L'ATLANTIQUE

MUSÉE DE LA MER

MUSÉE DE PRÉHISTOIRE Pl. Chapelle, Carnac, west of Vannes.
■ 1000-1200, 1400-1800 Wed.-Mon. (Sep.-June). ● 30F.
Finds from digs near Carnac; details on megaliths and standing stones.

MUSÉE DES POUPÉES 3 rue des Trente, Josselin. ■ 1000-1200,
1400-1800 Mar.-mid Nov.; Wed., Sat. & Sun., mid Nov.-Mar. ● 30F.
A display of 500 enchanting old dolls. See **VANNES-EXCURSION 3**.

MUSÉE DE LA VILAINE MARITIME Château des Baisses
Fosses, La Roche-Bernard, southeast of Vannes. ■ 1000-1200, 1400-
1800 June-Sep.; Sat. & Sun., Oct.-May. ● 25F.
*Maritime traditions of the people of Vilaine. See the models of local
ships.*

MUSÉE DE L'ATLANTIQUE La Citadelle, Port-Louis, west of
Vannes. ■ 1000-1200, 1400-1800 Wed.-Mon. Closed Nov. ● 30F.
History of French Compagnie des Indes; also a maritime museum.

MUSÉE DE LA RÉSISTANCE BRETONNE St. Marcel,
Malestroit, northeast of Vannes. ■ 0930-1200, 1400-1800. ● 30F.
*Shows aspects of the Maquis resistance and army vehicles in a 6 hectare
park. Note the Atlantic wall blockhouse, Sherman tank and 88 mm anti-
aircraft gun. See* **VANNES-EXCURSION 3**.

MUSÉE NICOLAZIC Opposite the basilica, Ste Anne-d'Auray, west
of Vannes. ■ 0800-2000 April-Oct. ● 20F.
Lifesize waxwork models of local citizens, linked to religious scenarios.

MUSÉE DE LA MER Lorient, west of Vannes.
■ 0900-1200, 1400-1800 Wed.-Mon. ● 20F.
History of the port of Lorient and its naval traditions.

LA CHOUANNERIE Plouharnel, west of Vannes.
■ 1000-1900 Tue.-Sun. (April-Sep.). ● 25F.
*Six large dioramas with 1000 clay figures, appropriately uniformed,
depicting the peasant revolt by Les Chouans (see* **A-Z**).

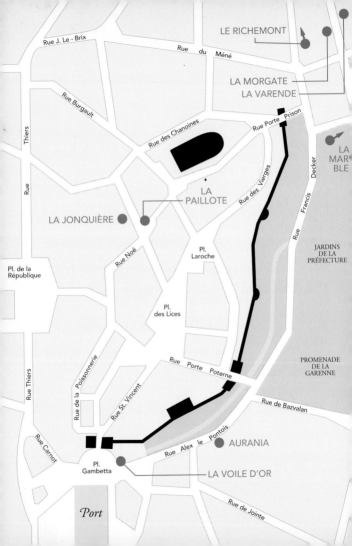

LE RICHEMONT

LA MORGATE
LA VARENDE

LA MAR-BLE

Rue J. Le - Brix

Rue du Méné

Rue Burgault

Rue des Chanoines

Rue Porte Prison

Rue Thiers

Rue

LA PAILLOTE

LA JONQUIÈRE

Rue des Vierges

Rue Francis

Rue Decker

JARDINS DE LA PRÉFECTURE

Rue Noé

Pl. Laroche

Pl. de la République

Pl. des Lices

PROMENADE DE LA GARENNE

Rue Porte Poterne

Rue de Bazvalan

Rue de la Poissonnerie

Rue St. Vincent

Rue Thiers

Rue Alex le Pontois

AURANIA

Rue Carnot

Pl. Gambetta

LA VOILE D'OR

Port

Rue de Jointe

Restaurants

LE RICHEMONT 26 pl. de la Gare. ■ 1200-1400, 2000-2130 Tue.-
Sat., 1200-1400 Sun. Closed Nov. & Feb. ● Expensive.
*Lobster, smoked salmon and foie gras specialities served in medieval sur-
roundings modelled on the 14thC chateau of Suscinio (see* **VANNES-
CASTLES & CHATEAUX***).*

LA VARENDE 22 rue de la Fontaine.
■ 1200-1400, 1915-2115 Mon.-Sat. ● Moderate.
A discreet gourmet restaurant. Try the special snail dish.

LA MARÉE BLEU 8 pl. Bir-Hakeim.
■ 1200-1400, 1930-2130. Closed mid Dec.-mid Jan. ● Moderate.
Restaurant with a good choice of prix fixe menus, including seafood.

LA JONQUIÈRE 9 rue des Halles.
■ 1200-2100. ● Moderate.
*In a half-timbered building. Try the hot goat's cheese and bacon salad, or
beef and lamb kebab in Roquefort sauce. Also has a salon de thé.*

LA VOILE D'OR 7 pl. Gambetta.
■ 1200-1400, 1900-2100. ● Moderate.
On 1st floor of hotel overlooking the port. Seafood and game in season.

AURANIA 12 rue Alex le Pontois.
■ 1200-1400, 1930-2130 Wed.-Mon. ● Moderate.
*In a handsome canopied house opposite the chateau gardens. Try
crevettes parfumées au Cognac (prawns) and the grilled dishes.*

LA MORGATE 21 rue de la Fontaine.
■ 1200-1400, 1900-2130 Mon.-Sat. ● Moderate.
Small restaurant in half-timbered house. The mullet is recommended.

LA PAILLOTE Rue des Halles.
■ 1200-1400, 1900-2230 Mon.-Fri., 1900-2230 Sat. ● Inexpensive.
*On the 1st floor overlooking a cobbled street. The Super Paillotte pizza
contains mussels. Try the coquilles St. Jacques (scallops) with cognac.*

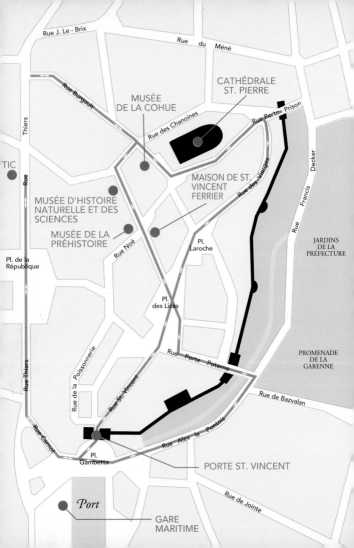

Duration: 2 hr.

Start at the tourist office, 1 rue Thiers (situated in the attractive 17thC Hôtel de Limur) and walk due east to Pl. Gambetta at the north end of the *gare maritime* (see **VANNES-ATTRACTIONS**). Turn left through the 18thC Porte St. Vincent into the old town and walk up Rue St. Vincent (the fish markets are just to the left), lined with attractive 18th-19thC houses and the Hôtel Dondel, which leads into the large Pl. du Poids Public where the fruit, flower and vegetable markets are held (Wed. & Sat. am). Note the turreted 17thC Hôtel de Francheville. Pl. des Lices is where 16thC tournaments, jousting matches and Breton wrestling took place, in what was originally the large medieval meadow near the ducal castle. Note the Hôtel de Marboeuf (Napoleon Bonaparte's sponsor) and the statue of St. Vincent. The markets here offer *sabots* (clogs), honeycomb and Breton jerseys – all interesting gifts. La Huche à Pain bakes 17 different kinds of bread including Gochthale Bretonne. Keep half right through Pl. Lucien Laroche to a small Y-junction. To the right is Rue des Vierges, from which leads the little Courtine de la Tour Juliette. There is a modern statue of St. Émilion, born in Vannes in the 8thC, with a bunch of grapes at his feet, and steps up to the ramparts. Turn left in Rue de la Bienfaisance. Before the brave citizens of the Revolution changed everything, this was the Rue des Trois Duchesses in honour of the three duchesses of Brittany who lived here (Catherine of Luxembourg, Isabel of Scotland and Françoise of Amboise). The Hôtel Sénant is dated 1680. At the end is the T-junction with Rue St. Gwenaël which runs alongside the cathedral. There are many timbered 14th-17thC houses with usually, alas, 20thC shops below. If you turn right you enter Pl. Brulée (rather sinister), Rue Porte Prison and the Port-Prison tower (even more sinister but rather photogenic). Turning left and then right into Pl. St. Pierre brings you to the Cathédrale St. Pierre (see **VANNES-ATTRACTIONS**), which is a glorious hotchpotch of architectural styles outside, and rich, indigestible ecclesiastical furnishings inside. No. 9 Pl. St. Pierre is early 15thC, one of the oldest houses in Vannes, and the high vaulted arcade houses the twin museums of the beaux-arts and history of the Golfe du Morbihan, known collectively as the Musée de la Cohue (see **VANNES-ATTRACTIONS**). Off Pl. St. Pierre are the medieval streets de la Monnaie and des Orfèvres. Further northwest

Cathédrale St. Pierre, Vannes

is Pl. Henri IV, originally called Colline de la Chèvre (where pagans worshipped goats), then with the Revolution, Pl. de la Liberté. With the restoration of the monarchy, its present name appeared. It is still lined with 15th-16thC half-timbered houses, three or four storeys high with overhanging façades. Look into Rue

Burgault and Impasse de la Palette. In the former is La Faïencerie, which sells delicate porcelain objects including lamps and violins, and in the latter Jeff de Bruges, selling the most enticing chocolates and *dragées* (sugared almonds). You will also see smart boutiques in this area. At the end of Rue Burgault is the large Pl. Maurice Marchais where the equestrian statue of Constable de Richemont guards the 19thC Renaissance-style Hôtel de Ville. Go back into Pl. Henri IV and right into Rue St. Salomon where No. 10 dates back to 1560. Turn left into Rue des Halles, once known as Rue Latine, where unruly students lived. The Hôtel de Roscanvel set back on the right houses the Musée d'Histoire Naturelle et des Sciences (0930-1200, 1400-1800 Mon.-Sat., mid June-mid Sep.; 15F), which has minerals and fossils as well as studies on migratory birds. La Taste Épicerie, opposite the Musée de la Cohue arcade, stocks multi-flavoured local honey, calvados and cider. Pl. Valencia has St. Vincent Ferrier's house of 1574 at No. 17 and on the corner of Rue Noé is the beautiful 15thC Château Gaillard, which houses the Musée de la Préhistoire (see **VANNES-ATTRACTIONS**). On the wall opposite are two wooden busts – Vannes and his wife – depicted as bucolic peasants. Rue Rogue (he was an unruly 18thC priest) leads back into Pl. des Lices but keep on past the Marché Couvert down Rue Porte Poterne and over the footbridge. The ramparts, towers, formal gardens and river are lovely. Turn right (facing you is the Promenade de la Garenne) into Rue Alex le Pontois which takes you back through Pl. Gambetta to the tourist office.

Anne de Bretagne: Daughter of Duke François II, Anne of Brittany married King Charles VIII in 1491 but remained duchess and sovereign of her native Brittany. The king died in 1498 and she returned to Brittany, but in the following year married King Louis XII (who had conveniently rid himself of his previous wife!). Popular with the Bretons and very religious, she made pilgrimages each year. She died in 1514 aged 37, with no male heir. Her daughter Claude inherited the Duchy of Brittany and married the future King François I.

Armorique, Parc Naturel Régional d': In Finistère, east, west and southeast of Brest, this huge nature park also includes Île d'Ouessant (see **Islands**) and other small islands. Huelgoat (see **A-Z**) is the best base from which to explore forests, hills, rivers and local *écomusées* along the many signposted trails. The park HQ is at the Domaine de Menez-Meur near Hanvec, southeast of Brest off the D 342. See **BREST-MUSEUMS**.

Arthurian Legends: The Celtic refugees from Ireland, Wales and Cornwall/Devon to 'Little Britain' at the end of the 5thC and during the 6thC brought magnificent folklore stories and legends with them which linger still. Cornouaille was supposedly occupied by members of King Arthur's court at Tintagel. The search for the Holy Grail (Joseph of Arimathea's cup) or Sangraal was undertaken by King Arthur and 50 Knights of the Round Table. The great forest of Brocéliande (modern Paimpont – see **VANNES-EXCURSION 3**) was the birthplace of Sir Lancelot. On the western edge is Trécesson, a splendid battlemented 14thC castle, set in the centre of a small lake, once the home of Sir Lancelot du Lac. The Château de Comper (see **RENNES-CASTLES & CHATEAUX**) was the birthplace of the fairy Viviane, known as the Lady of the Lake, who took Arthur's sword when he died. Viviane was in love with Merlin, King Arthur's wizard. To stop him leaving her she imprisoned him in the Perron de Merlin (magician's footprints) beside the spring at Barenton in the Val-sans-Retour. Morgane the witch lived under the rocks in this valley called the Rocher des Faux Amants, where she punished unfaithful knights. Sir Lancelot and the knight Percival were pure in heart and broke her spell. South of the forest is the river bridge called Pont du

Secret where Queen Guinevere told Sir Lancelot of her love for him. In the little church of Tréhorenteuc (off the D 141) paintings and mosaics illustrate the Knights of the Round Table and the Holy Grail. Further afield to the east, the powerful castle of Fougères (see **RENNES-CASTLES & CHATEAUX**) has a 14thC tower named La Mélusine after a fairy of the Arthurian legends. Perhaps Malory's *Morte d'Arthur* will provide your family with appropriate background before a visit to Brittany (and Cornouaille in particular). They will also enjoy the son et lumière 'Legends of the Round Table' at Forteresse de Largoët (see **VANNES-CASTLES & CHATEAUX**) during the summer.

Auray/St. Goustan: 18 km west of Vannes. Pop: 10,000. The attractive tidal river Loc'h or Auray separates Auray on the hilltop from the Riviera-style inland port of St. Goustan. Cobbled streets, churches, a stone bridge, riverside walks, exhibitions, strolling players and 15thC houses make this town well worth a visit. There are historical links with Benjamin Franklin, the 18thC Chouans (see **A-Z**) and the battle of 1364 which Du Guesclin (see **A-Z**) lost. Vedettes Vertes sail south into the Golfe du Morbihan. The restaurant L'Armorique is recommended and Le Relais Benjamin Franklin, 8 quai de Franklin, is an excellent creperie. See **VANNES-EXCURSION 2**.

Brest: 75 km north of Quimper. Pop: 160,000. Market days: Mon. & Fri. Brest is the second-largest city in Brittany and situated in the north-west corner of France. Almost totally destroyed in World War II (see **A-Z**), the large modern city which rose from the ashes is still France's major naval port and an important commercial and industrial centre. A commendable attempt has been made to restore the few architectural sites remaining from the 1944 bombardments. Brest has over 20 hotels (many inexpensive), a number of seafood restaurants, and is a good excursion centre to visit the Parc Naturel Régional d'Armorique and to make a tour of the fascinating parish closes between Landernau and Morlaix. See **BREST**.

Breton Boats: There are 50 types of traditional Breton boats ranging from the *bisquine* of Cancale, the Rance lighter, the Trégor *lugget* and the *flambart* of Locquémeau to the sloop of Iroise and the tunny boats of Dundée.

Breton Costume: If you attend a pardon (see **A-Z**) look closely at the traditional finery of the Breton costume. The men wear embroidered waistcoats and felt hats with ribbons, and the ladies have richly decorated aprons of velvet or satin, probably edged with lace, and often a bib. However, it is their white lace headdresses (*coiffes*), with lace collar and perhaps ribbons, which are so special. The Breton traditions of language (see **A-Z**), dress and customs are strongest in the west (Finistère and Morbihan) and the folklore museums at Quimper, Rennes and Dinan have good costume collections.

Breton Flag: The white and black Breton flag, known as Gwenn na Du, will often be seen. The five black stripes stand for the bishoprics of Haute-Bretagne and the four white for those of Basse-Bretagne. The top left-hand corner of the flag has eleven heraldic devices on a white background.

Cancale: 14 km east of St. Malo. Pop: 4700. A picturesque fishing port and seaside resort with the church of St. Méen and the Musée des Arts et Traditions Populaires (1000-1200 Tue.-Sun., 1500-1900 all week, July-mid Sep.; 15F). The Continental and Phare are two restaurants overlooking the port which sell oysters. Just north of the town is the Pointe de Grouin nature reserve, from where there are superb views along the coast.

Alignement de Menec, Carnac

Carnac: 34 km west of Vannes. Pop: 4000. Carnac is at the mainland end of the Quiberon peninsula. It has a fine 2 km-long beach and excellent Musée de Préhistoire/Miln le Rouzic (see **VANNES-MUSEUMS**), but is famous for the fan-shaped series of megalithic *alignements*, tumuli and dolmens within walking distance to the north. There are 17 different sites with over 4000 individual stones or boulders, some 4 m high. The three *alignements* are called Menec, Kerlescan and Kermario, the tumuli St. Michel, Kercado and Moustoir, and the dolmens Keriauac and Mané-Kerioned. There are more megaliths 8 km northwest near the D 781 to Lorient, including two *alignements* and four groups of dolmens and menhirs. Ask for a plan of the megaliths at the tourist office in Rue Brizeux, tel: 98930442, then visit the museum for a preview. See **VANNES-EXCURSION 2**.

Cartier, Jacques (1491-1557): An intrepid mariner and explorer from St. Malo, who in 1534 sailed across the Atlantic in search of gold, hoping to land in Newfoundland or Labrador. He took possession of the land he reached, which was the entrance to the St. Lawrence River. However, he thought he had reached an Asian river. He named the country Canada ('village' in Red Indian Huron language). See the Musée d'Histoire de la Ville (see **ST. MALO-ATTRACTIONS**) for details of Cartier's life, and also visit his house (see **St. Malo**).

Chateaubriand, François-René (1768-1848): The great Romantic writer was born in St. Malo. He spent two years in Combourg (see **DINAN-CASTLES & CHATEAUX**), and went to school in Dinan, Dol-de-Bretagne, Rennes and Brest; his six-volume *Mémoires d'Outre-tombe* recalls his childhood. From 1822-24 he was the ambassador in London but returned to France and wrote his epic *Les Martyrs*. He died in 1848 and was buried on the Île de Grand Bé off St. Malo. His portrait, by Girodet, hangs in the Musée d'Histoire de la Ville (see **ST. MALO-ATTRACTIONS**).

Chouans: The French Revolution was not to everybody's liking. The religious traditions of the Bretons were threatened, mass conscription for the Revolutionary armies drained Brittany of its young men, and priests were persecuted and many deliberately drowned in the Loire near Nantes.
In response, in 1793 the Chouans emerged (*chat-huant* is a screech owl). They wanted independence from Paris and rashly allied themselves with émigré royalists. Despite the help of a Royal Navy fleet, defeats followed at Carnac and Quiberon in 1793, though La Roche-Bernard was taken by the Chouan army. When Georges Cadoudal, an energetic leader who tried to kidnap Napoleon, was caught and executed in 1804, the Chouan revolt fizzled out.

Concarneau: 24 km southeast of Quimper. Pop: 18,000. The *raison d'être* of Concarneau is fish. The town is France's third-largest fishing port, with fishing museums, canneries, an auction market (*criée*) and harbours. However, it is the medieval Ville Close in the centre of the main port which really merits a visit. There are 11 hotels and many superb fish restaurants. See **QUIMPER-EXCURSION 2**.

Concarneau

Corsairs: For several hundred years the English Channel or La Manche was the hunting ground of pirates operating from the Devon and Cornwall coast and from the Breton ports of Roscoff, Morlaix and St. Malo. The privateers sometimes acted on their own freebooting initiative, preying on any ship smaller or less well armed than themselves. But frequently they were officially licensed by the appropriate monarch under Letters of Marque, whereby one-tenth of the proceeds went to the royal coffers, about two-thirds to the ship's owners, and the rest to the skipper and his corsair crew. The British had Drake and Hawkins, and the French had René Duguay-Trouin (1670-1736) and Jean Bart who sailed out of Morlaix and helped make the town wealthy. The English called St. Malo the 'Pirates' Nest' and even now the French proudly call it Ville des Corsairs. Robert Surcouf (1772-1827) was one of the most notorious. Important passengers who were captured were ransomed for large sums – crossing the Channel became a most hazardous undertaking! The Musée d'Histoire de la Ville (see **ST. MALO-ATTRACTIONS**) houses many intriguing records of the corsairs.

Dinan: 30 km south of St. Malo. Pop: 14,000. Market days: Thu. & Sat. Dinan probably ranks as the most attractive town in Brittany, with its fairy-tale medieval castle, 3 km of ramparts, promenades, parks, a fine 12th-17thC basilica and a small port. Well-kept, with trees and gardens, you will need to walk the cobbled streets and little squares to see the best of this enchanting, and pleasantly inexpensive, town. The hotels De France and La Caravelle are modestly priced and have good restaurants. Many excursions are possible by boat north and south, or inland to Bécherel, Combourg and Dol-de-Bretagne. See **DINAN**.

Dinard: West of St. Malo (14 km by road) across the bay. Pop: 10,000. Market days: Tue., Thu. & Sat. Dinard retains much of the Edwardian style of *la belle époque.* Many large and elegant houses and villas in the northern district of St. Enogat stand amid fig and palm trees, redolent of the Anglo-American era at the turn of the century. A plaque on the main promenade, erected in 1936, commemorates the centenary of the arrival of the first British residents in Dinard. The superb beach, seawater *piscines,* hotels, restaurants, museum, discos and casino make Dinard the smart, and therefore more expensive, Brittany resort. There are 7.5 km of fine seaside walks called Les Sentiers du Littoral between the beach at St. Enogat and the Barrage de la Rance, and son et lumière (see **A-Z**) shows take place at night over the promenade. Visit Pointe de Vicomte, Moulinet or Étetés, all within walking distance, or catch a vedette to Cap Fréhel, Île de Cézembre, Dinan or St. Malo. See **DINARD**.

Dol-de-Bretagne: 24 km southeast of St. Malo. Pop: 5000. The town is dominated by its huge granite 12th-13thC cathedral. Note the 13thC stained-glass window, tomb of Thomas James, the English Bishop of Dol (1482-1504), chapel of Ste Marguerite with her enchained demon, the dozen silver plaques illustrating the stations of the Cross, and two fine porches. During the Revolution it was turned into a stables and thus saved from damage. Next door in the 16thC treasury is the excellent Musée de Trésor (20F), with four 15thC cannon and armour outside, which depicts local history and folklore. In Grande Rue des Stuarts are the tourist office, a plaque commemorating the links between the Scottish Fitzalan family and the dukes and counts of

Brittany, and a dozen medieval houses. Look for the 11thC Les Petits Palets, 13thC Maison de la Guillotière (which houses a small museum of wooden statues of Breton saints) and the 16thC Hôtel de Monseigneur de Plédran. A score of medieval houses can also be found in Rue le Jamptel and Rue Ceinte. The Hôtel-Restaurant de Bretagne in Pl. Chateaubriand offers excellent-value accommodation and food. Mini-excursions from Dol-de-Bretagne include: the Promenade des Douves (moated public gardens north of the cathedral); Mont-Dol, a granite mount 4.5 km northwest and 'twinned' with Mont-St.-Michel; the 9 m-tall Menhir de Champ-Dolent 1.5 km south off the D 795; 15thC Château de Landal 12 km southeast, and Château des Ormes 8 km south off the D 795; and the Musée de la Paisannerie 4 km south on the D 795.

Du Guesclin, Bertrand (c. 1320-1380): Brittany's most famous citizen was born near Dinan. He became a great general who harried the English armies unmercifully from 1356 until his death. Despite being taken prisoner three times, this hero of scores of battles became Duke of Molina, King of Granada and High Constable of France. See his portrait in the Musée de Bretagne (see **RENNES-ATTRACTIONS**).

Fougères: 50 km northeast of Rennes. Pop: 25,000. An attractive town overlooking the river Nançon which winds through the centre. The castle (see **RENNES-CASTLES & CHATEAUX**), part 12thC, with 13 towers, ramparts and keep, and the old quarter, two museums and Gothic churches make Fougères a most agreeable stop. There are four hotels and two good restaurants – Les Voyageurs, 10 pl. Gambetta and Au Cellier, 29 rue Victor Hugo.

Fougères

Gauguin, Paul (1848-1903): In 1888 Gauguin joined a small group of American painters and went to Pont-Aven (southeast of Quimper) because it was cheap, the scenery was inspiring and the locals were prepared to sit for him inexpensively. His *Breton Country Women* is in the Musée d'Orsay in Paris, showing two coiffed peasants wearing aprons and colourful dresses against a Breton landscape of green fields, woods, a cottage and boulders. He lived in a manor house called Lezaven and sought inspiration in the Hôtel des Voyageurs. The next year he moved to Le Pouldu which he found more peaceful and from there he travelled to Tahiti. The Musée de Gauguin (see **QUIMPER-MUSEUMS**) has paintings from the Pont-Aven School (see **A-Z**).

Gradlon, King: About the time of the 6thC Arthurian legends (see **A-Z**), the town of Ys or Is was the capital of Cornouaille, with Gradlon as its monarch. A rather complicated legend involves the Devil in the form of a handsome young man and Gradlon's daughter Dahut, who was beautiful but wayward. She was persuaded to steal the king's key to the floodgates which protected Ys from the ocean and the city sank beneath the waves in Douarnenez bay. Father and daughter escaped on horseback, chased by the incoming waves, until a heavenly voice suggested that if he jettisoned his demon-daughter Gradlon would be saved. So she was drowned and turned into a wicked mermaid who, by her siren beauty, lured sailors to their doom in buried Ys. When Mass is celebrated on Good Fri. in a church below the waves, it is just possible she will be pardoned! King Gradlon founded a new capital at Kemper-Odetz (modern Quimper, 20 km southeast) and a statue of him on his trusty steed stands between the towers of the cathedral.

Huelgoat: 67 km east of Brest. Pop: 2000. This small town is in the heart of the unexplored countryside of the Parc Naturel Régional d'Armorique (see **A-Z**) and near the Arrée mountains. Try the Hôtel-Restaurant du Lac, Rue Général de Gaulle, which has river trout, lake perch and carp on the menu.

Islands: There are 13 islands – the 'string of pearls' – off Brittany which are permanently occupied, besides scores of others which are populated only by gannets and other bird life.
Chausey: Ferry from St. Malo, Cancale or Granville (in Normandy). Grande Île is 2 km in circumference and has two small forts, and a fishing village with the Hôtel-Restaurant du Fort et des Îles.
Bréhat: Ferry from St. Quay-Portrieux, Paimpol, Erquy, Dahouet and Binic. The island has a circumference of 3.5 km and a population of about 500. The ubiquitous Vauban linked the two main islands together with a bridge. The island was British-owned in the 15th-16thC and has several good beaches, a mild climate and lovely flora. Two lighthouses and many well-signed walks make this a popular resort.
Batz: Ferry from Roscoff. The island is 3.5 km in circumference and has a population of about 750. It is a farming and fishing community, with seaweed considered a 'crop'. The port of Kernoc'h is dominated by the lighthouse and sea rescue station. The island has a mild climate, some good beaches, the church of St. Pol and a pardon (see **A-Z**) on 26 July.
Ouessant (Ushant): Ferry from Brest. Ouessant is shaped like a crab and is in the western sector of the Parc Naturel Régional d'Armorique (see **A-Z**), with a population of 1200, and is roughly 8 km long and 4 km

Roscoff

wide. Because of the Gulf Stream,
Ouessant has mild winters and migrant
birds use it as a staging post. Three
lighthouses warn ships of the treacher-
ous Finistère coast. The island has roads
and a taxi service, a museum (see **BREST-
MUSEUMS**), unusual stone crosses
(*proella*) and a *centre ornithologique*.
Sein: Ferry from Audierne. The island is
small and flat with a population of 600.
As well as two lighthouses, a small port
and a lobster farm, there is also the village of Le Bourg, with its church, hotel
and four little restaurants noted for their ragout of lobster and potatoes.
Glénan: Ferries from Bénodet, Beg-Meil, Concarneau, Loctudy and
Forêt-Fouesnant. A group of nine small, barely inhabited islands. St.
Nicolas is the main island, while three of the others are part of a sea
navigation and sailing centre. Other islets are bird sanctuaries with

117

cormorants, gulls and terns. Penfret has a lighthouse, and on St. Nicolas is a rare narcissus brought by the Phoenicians 2000 years ago.

Groix: Ferry from Lorient. With a population of over 4000 and an area of 1770 hectares, Groix is now a sophisticated little resort. Port-Tudy is used by trawlers and has a summer marina, and the main town, Groix, has two hotel-restaurants, two camp sites, two restaurants and two creperies. There are half a dozen beaches, an *écomusée*, riding school and organized nature rambles. A network of roads links a dozen charming little hamlets, including Locmaria, with the fishing harbour.

Belle-Île: Ferry from Port Maria, Quiberon. The largest and most sophisticated Breton island, Belle-Île is 20 km in length and has a population of 5000. There is a small airport with planes from Quiberon and Lorient, an 18-hole golf course, riding centre, several yachting clubs, a sailing school, three marinas and an interesting museum in Vauban's citadel at Le Palais (1000-1200, 1400-1700; 30F). The west side of the island faces the Atlantic, with the Port Coton needles, similar to those off the Isle of Wight, several small ports, a large lighthouse and rocky creeks. The eastern side is more protected and has half a dozen fine sandy beaches. See **VANNES-EXCURSION 2.**

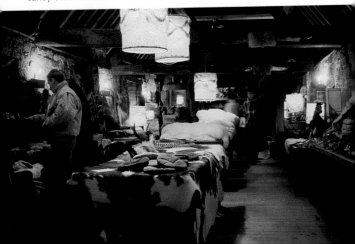

Locronan: 17 km north of Quimper. Pop: 6000. All cars and buses must park outside. The town is known as a *cité médiévale* and has a lovely cobbled main square. The 15thC church has the tomb of St. Ronan, a pilgrimage casket chapel, 'naïve' statues, an entombment frieze, and sculptures of biblical stories around the pulpit. The simple 16thC church of Notre Dame de Bonne Nouvelle, with a fountain and calvary, is 250 m down a lane to the north. Interesting crafts include *savonnerie de Bretagne* (soap), *cuirs et peaux* (leatherwork), *gâteaux bretons*, gravures of Breton legends, ironwork and pottery, all of which make pleasant souvenirs. Also see the Maison des Artisans, and the Musée des Peintures, Arts et Traditions in the small tourist office. The Hôtel-Restaurant Auberge du Prieuré offers *poulet au cidre*, and the Au Fer à Cheval *moules marinières*. Locronan is a superb village; try to visit out of season to enjoy it at its best. See **QUIMPER-EXCURSION 1**.

Lorient: 54 km west of Vannes. Pop: 65,000. Market days: Wed. & Sat. A major dockyard, fishing port and naval base, Lorient was extensively damaged in World War II (see **A-Z**). As a result the new town has little character, apart from its Keroman fishing port. Lorient has 22 hotels, many inexpensive restaurants and can be used as a base for excursions to the Île de Groix, west to Pont-Aven and Quimperlé, by river inland to Pontivy, and east to Carnac and Auray.

Lorient

Morlaix: 59 km east of Brest. Pop: 19,500. Market day: Sat. Morlaix is a minor port with a 15thC Vieille Ville on the estuary of the river Dorsen, and in the 16th-18thC was the home of various infamous pirates (see **Corsairs**). The town is now the centre of the Breton tobacco industry and the large factory at Quai de Léon can be visited (Wed. pm). The parish close circuit and Parc Régional Naturel d'Armorique are both within easy reach. See **BREST-EXCURSION**.

Paimpol: 45 km northwest of St. Brieuc. Pop: 8500. Market day: Tue. A modern fishing port and marina, oyster farming and vegetables have made Paimpol prosperous. The Musée de la Mer, the Abbaye de Beauport 2 km southeast and the harbour are all of interest. There is also a score of beaches within a few kilometres, plus boat trips to Île de Bréhat (see **Islands**). A pardon (see **A-Z**) is held on the 1st Sun. in Dec. See **ST. BRIEUC-EXCURSION**.

Pardons: One legacy of the 6thC influx into Brittany of Welsh, Irish and West Country evangelists has been the continuing deep religious beliefs of the countryfolk. This has been reflected in the traditional religious processions called pardons which started in the 16thC. The Catholic Church granted full indulgences for the Feast of the Virgin Mary and the Saints, thereby 'pardoning' all the sins that the faithful had committed. Pardons take place mainly in Finistère and, to a lesser extent, in Morbihan and Côte d'Armor. Wearing colourful costumes, the worshippers process – sometimes led by a bishop – from the central square to the church. Nearly every small village and town has its own procession, where pilgrims sing hymns, and statues, banners and candles are carried by men, girls and priests. The largest and most popular pardons are now great fêtes and tourist attractions, since after the service of the Blessed Sacrament is over, the feasting and fun commence. People partake of crepes (see **Food**) and cider, and old dances (*fest-noz*) are performed to music played on bagpipes (*cornemuses*) and oboes (*bombardes*). There might also be a fall or two of traditional Breton wrestling (*ar gouren*), in which the wrestlers kiss each other three times before battle gets under way. If you take part in a (religious) pardon, you should dress appropriately. See **Breton Costume**.

Parish Closes: In the 16thC Breton merchants – perhaps out of guilt – vied with each other to have built the most comprehensive and beautiful parish church close, usually in the centre of the village. Architects were briefed carefully to build a monumental arch symbolizing passing from life on earth into the kingdom of death, to Paradise and life eternal. The *enclos paroissial* also needed a church, cemetery, charnel house (where bodies were dismembered and the bones placed in an ossuary) and calvary, all surrounded by a high wall. Ideally, the merchant, priest and stonemason would try to produce a balance but this was rarely achieved. A magnificent calvary may be found in one *enclos* but perhaps no triumphal arch, a meagre enclosing wall and a modest ossuary. Calvaries built in granite emphasized the death of Christ on a central cross, with the two thieves on either side (also on crosses), a group of Roman guards and the Virgin Mary. The ornate friezes are superb: Guimiliau has 200 figures, Plougastel-Daoulas 180 and Pleyben many more. The Last Supper, the Washing of the Disciples' Feet, the Visitation, the Nativity and the Adoration of the Shepherds are frequently sculpted, and each *calvaire* should be closely scrutinized to identify the biblical story.

The majority of parish closes are to be found in Finistère. Near Brest there are fine groups at Pencran, Plougastel-Daoulas, Argol, Sizun, Commana, Plounéour-Menez, La Marture, Guimiliau, Ploudiry, Lampaul-Guimiliau, Pleyber-Christ, St. Thégonnec, Plougonven and Berven. Around Quimper they can be found at Forêt-Fouesnant, Kerlaz, St. Vennec, Pleyben, Brasparts, Cleden-Poher, St. Hernin, Lannérdern, La Roche-Maurice and Loquefret, and further east at Kergrist-Moelou. See **BREST-EXCURSION**.

Pont-Aven School (1886-91): This small town southeast of Quimper inspired a school of painters including Paul Gauguin (see **A-Z**), Emile Bernard, Charles Laval, Paul Sérisier and Maurice Denis, and the English graphic artist, Ralph Caldecott. Many other Impressionists came to Brittany to paint: Eugène Boudin, Camille Corot, Auguste Renoir, Odilon Redon, Eugène Isabey and more were duly inspired by Douarnenez, Audierne, Penmarc'h, Pont-l'Abbé and Quimperlé, as well as Pont-Aven, Concarneau and Le Pouldu. An exhibition of paintings from the Pont-Aven School is held in the Musée de Gauguin (see **QUIMPER-MUSEUMS**) during the summer.

Moulin de Rosmadel, Pont-Aven

Pontivy: 52 km north of Vannes. Pop: 14,000. Market day: Mon. The Welsh monk St. Ivy built the first bridge here in the 6thC, hence Pontivy's name. The river Blavet flows through the town which is a curious mixture of 16th-17thC half-timbered houses around Pl. du Martray, and the 'new town' of Napoléonville built by Bonaparte in 1806. The 15thC chateau and 11thC church of Notre Dame de la Joie are both worth a visit. There are six hotels, of which the Hôtel-Restaurant Chez Robic, 2 rue Jean Jaurès, offers excellent value. Excursions are possible through the rural heart of Brittany to Josselin, Mur-de-Bretagne, Loudeac and the gorges to the northwest. See **VANNES-EXCURSION 3**.

Quimper: 76 km southeast of Brest. Pop: 60,000. Market days: Wed. & Sat. The *préfecture* town of Finistère, it is the meeting place of two rivers, the Odet and Steir. An inland town situated in a pretty valley, Quimper has the beach resorts of Pont-l'Abbé, Bénodet and Concarneau 15-20 km due south. The Vieille Ville, Gothic cathedral, some fine museums and the famous faïence (pottery) make the town an

Quimper

interesting visit. Quimper has 15 hotels, many inexpensive, and its restaurants rank among the best in Brittany. The Festival de Cornouaille, held in late July, is the ideal chance to see Breton culture and traditions in dress, music and dance. Besides boat trips south on the river Odet, there are excursions east to see the 'painting' of Pont-Aven, the Breton folklore centre of Douarnenez, and the Parc Régional Naturel d'Armorique to the north. See **QUIMPER**.

Quimperlé: 46 km east of Quimper. Pop: 12,000. Market day: Fri. An under-estimated town bisected by the rivers Ellé and Isole, it has two notable churches, a folklore museum and a small old quarter. Bluebeard's forest of Carnoët is 5 km due south. See **QUIMPER-EXCURSION 2**.

Rennes: 52 km south of Dinan. Pop: 200,000. Market days: Daily. Rennes is the capital of Brittany and *préfecture* of Ille-et-Vilaine. An unfortunate fire in 1720 destroyed much of the medieval city but Rennes is still well worth a visit to see its Palais de Justice, Hôtel de Ville, two fine museums, Cathédrale St. Pierre and other inter-esting churches, and the Jardin du Thabor. Two universities and nearly 30,000 enrolled students keep this prosperous city young at heart. There are many good-quality restaurants and Rennes makes an ideal centre for excursions to Vitré and Fougères to the east, chateaux to the north, and the Paimpont forest to the west. The Canal d'Ille et Rance runs through the city and half- or full-day cruises can be taken on the *bateaux-mouches* to Dinan and St. Malo to the north and Redon and the Atlantic coast to the south. See **RENNES**.

Ste Anne d'Auray

Roscoff: 65 km northeast of Brest. Pop: 4000. Arrivals from Plymouth or Cork on cross-Channel ferry services get their first taste of Brittany as they enter this fishing and commercial port, once the haunt of corsairs (see **A-Z**), which has two unusual claims to fame. The first is its links with Scotland: Mary Stuart, the future Queen of Scots, landed here in 1548, and almost two centuries later, after Culloden, Bonnie Prince Charlie sought shelter. The second is that 70 varieties of seaweed are commercially harvested along the Roscoff coast – an unusual crop! It is a good resort with several beaches close by, and has 13 hotels and many restaurants including Le Bellevue, Rue Jeanne d'Arc, which has *huitres chaudes florentine* (oysters) on the menu. Boat cruises go to Île de Batz, and inland are St. Pol-de-Léon, Morlaix and the parish close circuit. See **BREST-EXCURSION**.

St. Brieuc: 54 km west of Dinan. Pop: 51,000. Market days: Wed., Fri. & Sat. The *préfecture* town of the Côte d'Armor department, St. Brieuc has the advantage of having a score of good beaches nearby on the Baie de St. Brieuc. There are several important festivals and fairs in the town, including the Michaelmas fair, a Breton folklore festival and pardon (see **A-Z**) in May, and a festival of Breton music in Sep., proving that local traditions are being kept alive in this part of the region. There are 16 hotels, a number of good restaurants, and a local cultural centre which organizes music, theatre and art events throughout the year. See **ST. BRIEUC**.

Ste Anne d'Auray: 18 km west of Vannes. Pop: 1600. The most important religious 'complex' in Brittany. Ste Anne, mother of the Virgin Mary, appeared to the farmer Yves Nicolazic in 1623 and a church was built on the spot, followed by a basilica, and now the little town has pilgrimages and pardons (see **A-Z**) from Mar. to Oct., with those of 26 July and 15 Aug. attended by thousands. In addition to the huge dominating basilica there are other important buildings, including the Trésor et Galerie d'Art (15F). The 17thC cloisters are presently being repaired. In the park the statue of Ste Anne stands over a 'miraculous' fountain, and the war memorial surmounted by the Croix de Jerusalem commemorates 250,000 Bretons who gave their lives in World War I. The Musée Nicolazic (see **VANNES-MUSEUMS**) has displays of Breton folklore and there is also the oratory or Accueil Spirituel, the La Scala Sancta steps and the Historial de Ste Anne. The hotel-restaurants Le Moderne and Boule d'Or offer sustenance to pilgrims and visitors. See **VANNES-EXCURSION 2**.

St. Malo: Pop: 47,000. Market days: Tue. & Fri. The town faces Dinard (14 km by road) across the mouth of the river Rance and now includes Paramé to the east and St. Servan to the south. Almost totally destroyed in 1944 (see **World War II**), a magnificent repair job has been done to reproduce the original medieval town and harbour, once the home of several notorious corsairs (see **A-Z**). The walled town, called the Intra Muros, the 13th-16thC castle, watchtowers and Cathédrale St. Vincent make St. Malo a most attractive visit. See also the offshore Fort National, Île de Grand Bé and the tall 14th-17thC Tour Solidor at St. Servan-sur-Mer (1000-1200, 1400-1800; 18F), plus the various ports and harbours. In Rothéneuf suburb is the Manoir de Jacques Cartier (1000-1200, 1400-1800 Wed.-Sun., June-Sep.; 20F). St. Malo has 48 hotels and many top-class restaurants, and excursions can be made to Mont St. Michel and Combourg. See **ST. MALO**.

Sévigné, Marquise de (1626-96): An elegant and distinguished woman with a glamorous and powerful series of lovers, she spent the last quarter of the 17thC writing her famous letters about her life at court and the provincial nobility and gentry, and spent much of her time from 1654 onwards at Les Rochers-Sévigné (see **RENNES-CASTLES & CHATEAUX, MUSEUMS**), which is now a literary shrine.

Tristan & Isolde: Wagner's opera was based on a legend involving Mark, King of Cornouaille, Tristan, Prince of Lyonesse (his nephew) and the beautiful Irish princess, Isolde (or Iseult). Mark intended to marry Isolde who fell in love with Tristan, with tragic results involving love philtres. There are a variety of endings, but Isolde, grieving, usually follows her lover to his grave. La Fontenelle was King Mark's palace at Douarnenez, and Tristan possibly lived on the offshore Île Tristan.

Vannes: 114 km southeast of Quimper. Pop: 46,000. Market days: Wed. & Sat. Vannes is the *préfecture* town of the Morbihan department. The multi-islanded Golfe du Morbihan immediately to the south and the elegant Vieille Ville, complete with ramparts, Cathédrale St. Pierre, museums and a major aquarium, make Vannes an interesting and attractive visit. Vannes has 20 hotels, many restaurants serving seafood, and a nearby camp site. The festival of Arvor is held by the ramparts on 15 Aug. Excursions are possible to the megaliths of Carnac and Gavrinus to the west, Quiberon and Belle-Île to the southwest, and a plethora of castles, including Josselin, to the north. See **VANNES**.

Vitré: 37 km east of Rennes. Pop: 13,500. This is certainly among the half dozen most attractive towns in Brittany, with an 11th-15thC chateau (see **RENNES-CASTLES & CHATEAUX**), medieval town, ramparts, the flamboyant Gothic church of Notre Dame and a museum, and the river Vilaine flowing gently through the centre. Vitré has six hotels and several good restaurants, including Le Pichet, Taverne de l'Écu and St. Yves.

World War II: From the summer of 1940, when the German armies overran France, until its deliverance four years later by the Americans, Brittany knew the agony of occupation. The long coastline became

Hitler's Atlantic wall, with concrete strongpoints, pillboxes and bunkers overlooking each port and mined beach. The Wehrmacht occupied the towns and the Luftwaffe used the airports to attack southwest England and Allied shipping in the Atlantic and Channel. The great naval dockyard at Brest, which was a base for the German fleet, and the submarine base at Lorient, became prime targets for the Allied bombers. By the time the Allies landed in Normandy in June 1944 the Breton resistance movement or Maquis numbered over 30,000. Their courageous sabotage of railways, barracks and factories slowed down the German war effort. After the great battles in Normandy the American tanks swept south through St. Lo and Avranches into Brittany and bottled up the Germans in St. Malo, Lorient, Brest and other towns. The enemy eventually surrendered but the heavy fighting and bombing destroyed the towns. St. Malo was in ruins but has been beautifully and lovingly restored to its original medieval beauty. Brest and Lorient had their original old towns destroyed to be replaced by humdrum busy cities with modern architecture. The Musée de la Résistance Bretonne (see **VANNES-MUSEUMS**) re-creates the Nazi occupation and the Breton resistance. See **BREST-ATTRACTIONS**.

Vannes

Accidents & Breakdowns: There are emergency telephones approximately every 20 km on main roads and these are connected direct to the local police stations which operate 24 hr a day. Motorists involved in a traffic accident must complete a *constat à l'amiable*, the blue and white European Accident Statement Form, before the vehicle is moved. If the vehicle has been seriously damaged, an expert's examination is advised prior to your return to the UK. The *constat à l'amiable* was introduced by the French insurance companies and it must be signed by the other party, but if a dispute arises and one of the parties involved should refuse to complete the *constat à l'amiable*, then the other party should immediately obtain a written report from a bailiff (*huissier*), which is known as a *constat d'huissier*. A bailiff can usually be found in any large town and charges a fee of 400F for preparing the report. Normally the police are only called out to accidents where persons are injured, a driver is under the influence of alcohol or the accident impedes the traffic flow.

If your vehicle breaks down, obtain local assistance as there is no countrywide motoring club road service in France. For assistance on a motorway telephone the *brigade de gendarmerie* from an emergency telephone or service station. The police will contact a garage for you but should it be necessary to remove the vehicle from the motorway for repair the choice of garage may be determined by the motorist. For AA members there is an emergency service, tel: 05302222 or 21872121. For RAC members, tel: 21963530, and motorists covered by a Europ Assistance policy, tel: 19-4416801234. The AA operates a port service in Calais, Boulogne and Cherbourg. See **Consulates**, **Driving**, **Emergency Numbers**.

Accommodation: Because of the popularity of the region, in midsummer in the main coastal resorts and towns of Brittany, it is advisable to book hotels or camp sites in advance. There are five categories of hotel: * (basic), ** (comfortable), *** (very comfortable), **** (high class) and ***** (luxury). A double room costs anything between 150F and 1500F per night. The cheaper, more basic hotels are usually near the railway and bus stations. You will find booking facilities at the main tourist offices in each town (see **Tourist Information**). They offer help

with last-minute difficulties but not necessarily the best deal. See **Camping & Caravanning, Canal Trips, Horse-drawn Carriages, Youth Hostels**.

Airports: Although there are eight airports in Brittany, Britair and Air France/Air Inter use only the following aerodromes: Britair, tel: 0293-502044, flies from Gatwick to Brest, Quimper and Rennes (as well as Caen and Le Havre), and from Cork to Brest and Quimper (as well as a direct flight to Nantes).
Air Inter, 158 New Bond St, London W1Y 0AY, tel: 081-7504484, flies from Heathrow to Brest and Quimper; from Birmingham to Brest, Lorient and Rennes; and from Heathrow, Aberdeen, Birmingham, Bristol, Cardiff and Manchester to Nantes.
In addition, Jersey Airlines, tel: 034-078400, flies to Dinard/St. Malo from Exeter, Bournemouth and Southampton.

Artisans: Two thousand craftsmen and women produce a wide variety of work for sale throughout the region, including cabinets and woodwork, ceramics, pottery and stone carvings, lace and embroidery, Breton dolls, woven fabrics, leatherware, fishermen's wool jumpers, jackets and pullovers. Locronan (see **A-Z**) is a good example of a small town with a range of interesting artisan crafts. In the Parc Naturel Régional d'Armorique, Ferme St. Michel at the foot of Mont St. Michel de Brasparts houses the Maison des Artisans, tel: 98814113.

Baby-sitters: Ask your hotel manager, chambermaid or, failing that, the local tourist office. Expect to pay 30F-50F per hr or 150F-200F per day. At camp sites or beach resorts, there are usually child-minding clubs. See **Children**.

Banks: See **Currency**, **Money**, **Opening Times**.

Best Buys: Ideas for souvenirs or presents include Breton lace head-dresses (*coiffes*), costumed Breton dolls, ceramics and faïence from Quimper, cider from Fouesnant, *sabot* (clogs), thick knitted fishermen's jerseys (*chandails bretons*), wickerwork baskets and handmade lace (*dentelle*). You may also be tempted by the local chocolates, confectionery, cakes, biscuits and pancakes (*galettes*), pralines from Rennes, and *berlingots* (boiled sweets). See **Artisans**, **Markets**, **Shopping**.

Bicycle & Motorcycle Hire: Most SNCF stations rent bicycles. Youth hostels will also rent bicycles at lower prices. Expect to pay c. 50F per day, with a deposit of 200F-300F, but a lower price for weekly rental.

Main hiring outlets:
Dinan: Scardin, 30 rue Carnot; Dinard: Briez Cycles, 8 rue de St.
Énogat; Quimper: Velodet, 4 bis av. de la Mer; Rennes: Hertz, Av. du
Mail; St. Malo: Rouxel, 12 av. Jean Jaurès.

Boats: Brittany has more boat (vedette) excursions available than any
other region in France. Most are into the Channel and ocean but others
are inland on canals and rivers. There is a bewildering choice and the
following list is just a selection. When in doubt consult your local
tourist office for advice, timings and current prices.
Brest: Le Fret, Île d'Ouessant, Molène and Île de Sein; Dinan: St. Malo
and Dinard; Quimper: River Odet; St. Malo: Return trips to Portsmouth,
Weymouth, Jersey, Guernsey, Sark, Cap Fréhel, St. Malo estuary and
Mont St. Michel, and one-way to the Côte d'Émeraude (Dinard, Dinan,
Île de Cézembre and Îles Chausey); Vannes: Belle-Île, Golfe du
Morbihan, river Auray and Île aux Moines.
See **Canal Trips**, **Islands**.

Budget:

Hotel breakfast	25F-50F
Restaurant prix fixe lunch	60F-450F

Plat du jour	30F-45F
Museum/chateau ticket	12F-30F
Bottle of *vin du patron*	40F-50F
Hotel room for two	150F-1500F
Picnic lunch for two from supermarket	60F

Buses: Bus stations (*gares routières*) and services are efficient and rel-
atively cheap. Many buses are run by the SNCF as a result of the clo-
sure of local railway lines. Bus stations are therefore usually near the
railway stations. Sun. services are much reduced. There are a number
of local bus services such as Tourisme Verney, Courriers Bretons,
Autocars Douguet, Vedettes Armoricaines, Cars de Cornouaille, Cars
Caoudal and Transports le Bayon. It may seem complicated but you
can get advice from the *gare routière*, the tourist office or your hotel
manager.
Main bus stations:
Brest: Av. Clemenceau; Dinan: Pl. de la Gare; Dinard: Pl. de la Gare
and Rue de la Corbinais; Quimper: Next to railway station; Rennes: Bd.
Magenta, off Pl. de la Gare; St. Brieuc: Bd. Waldeck-Rousseau;
St. Malo: Esplanade St. Vincent; Vannes: Next to railway station.

Cameras & Photography: Films, video cassettes and flashes are
easily available in towns throughout Brittany. Check with staff before
using a camera in museums or art galleries, as you will find there are
usually restrictions.

Camping & Caravanning: Brittany has 700 camp sites averaging
about 100 places per site. They are run to high standards, many by the
local council, and a number are members of Les Campings de l'Union
Bretonne. There are six categories of price/comfort: AN is *aire
naturelle* (basic but with regulated facilities); CF refers to camp sites on
farms; and there are also one-, two-, three- and four-star sites.
Campings-Caravaning is a yearly brochure, available from the larger
tourist offices, giving comprehensive details on camp sites. For a complete list of camp sites, consult the French Government Tourist Office,
178 Piccadilly, London, W1V 0AL, tel: 071-4996911.

Canal Trips: With some 600 km of navigable canals and rivers in Brittany, an inland 'nautical' holiday should be considered. There are four main routes: north–south from St. Malo or Dinan along the Canal d'Ille et Rance to Rennes, then by the river Vilaine to Redon, La Roche-Bernard and the sea; segments of the Canal de Nantes à Brest from Port-Launay via Châteaulin, Pleyben and Châteauneuf-du-Faou to Carhaix-Plouguer; the canalized river Blavet from Lorient to Hennebont, Baud and Pluméliau; and the section from Pontivy to Redon via Rohan, Josselin and Malestroit. There is a wide choice of boats with a capacity of 2-10 people, for hire for weekends or a full week. The charges vary according to the season, July and Aug. being double that of the low season. A deposit is required of c. 2000F for a boat. There are also larger vedettes for 65 people from which you can sightsee on 2 hr trips, or you could hire a canoe/kayak and stay at a camp site or hotel. Tourist offices will be able to advise you where to rent. See **Boats**.

Car Hire: Every town in Brittany offers competitive car rental services from the major international operators as well as local (and therefore possibly cheaper) firms. To hire a car you must produce a passport and a current driving licence which has been valid for at least one year. A cash deposit is necessary or payment by credit card, and proof of a local (hotel) address. Check that your hire contract specifies whether the rates are per kilometre, per day or per week with unlimited mileage, and that tax (TVA) is included. Ensure that you are fully covered for all risks with a comprehensive policy, including a green card. The minimum age is 21-25, depending on the company. Lower rates in Brittany will probably be available out of season.

Main car rental outlets:

Brest: Avis, 3 bd. des Français Libres, tel: 98446302; Hertz, 14 rue Colbert, tel: 98801151. Dinan: Dinan Auto Service, Rue de la Violette, tel: 96850852. Dinard: Avis, Aéroport de Pleurtuit, tel: 99462520; Europcar, tel: 99467570. Quimper: Europcar, 12 rue de Concarneau, tel: 98900068; Avis, 8 av. de la Gare, tel: 98903134. Rennes: Citer, 14 rue Tronjolly, tel: 99306900; Europcar, 56 av. du Mail, tel: 99595056; Budget, 11 rue de la Santé, tel: 99651321. St. Brieuc: Avis, 2 bd.

Clemenceau, tel: 96334414; Europcar, 11 bd. Charner, tel: 96944545.
St. Malo: Europcar, 16 bd. des Talards, tel: 99567517; Thrifty, 46 bd. de
la République, tel: 99564760. Vannes: Europcar, 46 av. Victor Hugo,
tel: 97424343.

Chateaux: The chateaux and fortresses of Brittany are not, in general,
as beautiful as those in the Loire valley, but there are a number of great
architectural interest. There are four which every visitor should try to
see: Vitré, Fougères, Josselin and St. Malo. See **CASTLES & CHATEAUX** topics for **DINAN, RENNES, ST. BRIEUC** and **VANNES**.

Chemists: There are plenty of chemists (*pharmacies*), identifiable by
a green cross sign, in all towns in Brittany. They are usually open 0900-
1930 Mon.-Sat. and have a Sun. rota which your hotel manager or
tourist office can advise. Each chemist has a notice in the window with
the addresses of those open at night. See **Health**.

Children: There are plenty of opportunities for keeping children
occupied; castles and chateaux, perhaps a parish close (see **A-Z**) and
certainly a visit to the sites of the Arthurian legends (see **A-Z**) and the
Breton corsairs' (see **A-Z**) activities. Megaliths and menhirs will intrigue
most children, as will the zoos at Branféré (east of Vannes), Trégomeur
(northwest of St. Brieuc), Pouldreuzic (west of Quimper) and Pont-
Scorff (north of Lorient). Visits to lighthouses (see **A-Z**) and certain
museums (Rennes car museum, the Brest and Camaret naval museums),
as well as *écomusées* and bird sanctuaries at Sizun, Cap Fréhel, Les
Sept Îles and La Brière, could be considered. In addition, there are fish
farms at Roscoff, Audierne and Primez, a butterfly park in Vannes, a salt
marsh museum at Batz-sur-Mer, botanical gardens in Combrit and
Brest, and the caves at Morgat to explore. Perhaps the national studs
(*haras*) at Hennebont and Lamballe, and the doll museums in Josselin
castle and St. Malo-Paramé will also be of interest. Older children will
enjoy visits to the glassworks in Locronan and faïence workshops in
Quimper, the Pleumeur-Bodou space telecommunications station and
the Rance valley tidal power scheme. There are also a score of man-
made *parcs de loisir*, including those at Locquirec-Trégamor, Laz,

Betton and Iffendic, with mini-golf, pony rides, animal parks and children's amusements. The local tourist office will advise you of the nearest attractions. See **Baby-sitters**.

Climate: This exposed northwest corner of France is bright and breezy with rain likely on average on alternate days so be prepared – and thankful when raincoats and anoraks are not needed. However, it is mild throughout the year thanks to the Gulf Stream. Average temperatures are 7-15°C (spring and autumn), 14-20°C (summer) and 4-10°C (winter), but in this large region there are bound to be considerable variations between inland towns and more exposed ports and harbours.

Complaints: It is very rare in Brittany to be overcharged in hotels or restaurants but nevertheless check every bill as you would at home. Ensure that if you have chosen a fixed-price menu (there may be several), the waiter knows which one you have selected. If you have a serious complaint take it immediately to the manager of the establishment. If you get no satisfaction go to the tourist office, and only as a final resort go to the police.

Consulates:

Hon. UK – La Hulotte, 6 av. de la Libération, Dinard, tel: 99462664.
UK – 6 rue Lafayette, Nantes, tel: 40485747.

Conversion Chart:

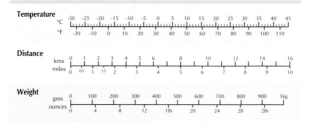

Crime & Theft: Special care should always be taken of handbags and wallets, credit cards, etc. Never leave your car unlocked and remove or hide any valuables. Report thefts immediately to the nearest police station and obtain an *attestation de vol* document so that you can claim insurance. Inform your consulate (see **A-Z**) at once if your passport is stolen. In emergencies, tel: 17; you will be put through to the local police station. See **Emergency Numbers**, **Insurance**, **Police**.

Currency: The French unit of currency is the franc, which is divided into 100 centimes. Banknotes are issued for 500F, 200F, 100F, 50F and 20F (the latter three will be replaced by coins in 1992-93). Coins are 10F, 5F, 2F, 1F, 50c, 20c, 10c and 5c. See **Money**.

Customs Allowances:

UK/EC	Cigarettes	Cigarillos	Cigars	Tobacco	Still Table Wine	Spirits/Liqueurs	Fortified Wine	Additional Still Table Wine	Perfume	Toilet Water	Gifts & Souvenirs
Duty Free	200 *or*	100 *or*	50 *or*	250 g	2 *l*	1 *l* *or*	2 *l* *or*	2 *l*	60 cc/ml	250 cc/ml	£32
Duty Paid	800	400	200	1 kg	90 *l* *	10 *l*	20 *l*				

* Of which no more than 60 l should be sparkling wine.

Since 1 Jan. 1993 restrictions on allowances for duty-paid goods brought into the UK from any EC country have been abolished. Travellers are now able to buy goods, including alcoholic drinks and tobacco, paying duty and VAT in the EC country where the goods are purchased. However, duty-paid goods should be for the traveller's own use and carried by him personally. Whereas previously there were either-or options, travellers can now bring back the sum of the goods in the duty-paid column.

Disabled People: For information about accommodation, transport, facilities and aids for the disabled, see the booklets *Touristes Quand Même* and *Guide des Transports à l'usage des Personnes à Mobilité Réduite* supplied by the tourist office. All TGV high-speed trains can accommodate wheelchairs, and guide dogs are transported free. Other trains have a special compartment and an escalator for boarding. See **Health**.

Drinks: In France there are no licensing laws, so you can buy alcohol in bars and cafés at any time. House wines are sold by the litre (*une carafe*), half litre (*un demi-litre*) or quarter litre (*un quart*); a jug (*un pichet*) can hold either a quarter or half litre. Beer is usually lager. At meals plain water (*une carafe d'eau*) comes free. Coffee: ask for *un café* for a small strong black espresso, *un café au lait* for coffee with milk, and *un grand crème* for a large white coffee. Tea is available at *salons de thé*, and hot chocolate is popular; ask for *un chocolat*. Drinks are less expensive served standing in a bar or café (*au comptoir*). A pavement table may cost more. In Brittany try the local ciders, a liqueur made at Plougaste, 'lambic' cider-liqueur, Chouchen honey liqueur and white Muscadet or Gros-Plant wines from the Nantes region.

Driving: Apart from the rush-hour traffic in Rennes and Brest, driving in Brittany is a pleasure, particularly out of season, and especially on the minor inland roads. You will need a valid UK or international driving licence plus comprehensive insurance documents (preferably a green card), a nationality sticker, yellow filters for headlamps and a red warning triangle. The French drive on the right-hand side of the road, and at T-junctions, intersections and roundabouts the traffic from the right has priority. The wearing of seat belts is compulsory for passengers in the front and recommended for those in the back. Try to make any long journeys by car on Sun. when trucks are forbidden by law. The speed limit in built-up areas is 60 kph; on main roads 90-100 kph; and on motorways (*autoroutes*) 130 kph. Speeding offences carry a large fine from motorway police – the fine is payable immediately. French drivers are very competitive, and a foreign numberplate is a challenge which you should resist. See **Accidents & Breakdowns**, **Car Hire**, **Parking**, **Petrol**.

Drugs: In France it is illegal to use or possess any form of narcotic and anyone caught trying to smuggle drugs into the country faces almost certain imprisonment.

Eating Out: By law all restaurants must display their prices outside and offer at least one fixed-price menu (*menu fixe, rapide menu, menu touristique*) as well as the à la carte. These fixed-price menus for two or three courses can cost as little as 50F, whereas the à la carte is always more expensive. The plat du jour is usually good, so ask the waiter what it is. Restaurants traditionally serve lunch from midday and rarely after 1400, and the evening meal from 1930-2100, but brasseries and bistros will serve a plat du jour at almost any time. Cafés serve a variety of drinks all day, as well as snacks, sandwiches and *croque-monsieur* (a toasted ham and cheese sandwich). Every tourist office will have a list of local restaurants, with addresses, telephone numbers, style of cuisine and some indication of price. In the topics section of this guide an Inexpensive three-course meal would cost 50F-100F, a Moderate meal 100F-200F and an Expensive meal over 200F. See RESTAURANTS topic page by town, **Food**.

HOMARD
BRETON
240,00 € Kg

Electricity: 220 V; a two-pin adaptor is required, available from most electrical shops.

Emergency Numbers:

Police   17
Fire brigade   18
Medical emergency   18
SAMU (24 hr ambulance)
Brest, tel: 98461133/98808050; Dinan, tel: 96392760; Dinard, tel: 99284315; Quimper, tel: 98901111; Rennes, tel: 99284315; St. Brieuc, tel: 99284315; St. Malo, tel: 99284315; Vannes, tel: 97426642.

Events: Tourist offices issue a list of local events. Every town has a series of events variously described as *fete votive* (after the patron saint), *spectacle, manifestation* or *animation*. A *foire* or fair will have a band, some dancing in the evening, roundabouts and probably some artisan stalls.

Pentecost: Quimperlé, Fête de Toulfouen.

July–August: St. Malo, Church music festival.

Mid-July: Dinan, Music festival, including Celtic harp competition.

2nd Sun. in July: Pont-l'Abbé, Fête des Brodeuses. *4th Sun. in July:* Paimpol, Newfoundland and Iceland festival.

1st Sun. in August: Pont-Aven, Festival des Fleurs d'Ajoncs (Golden Gorse). *Early August:* Vannes, Festival de Jazz and Journées Medievales (troubadours and tournaments). *3rd Sun. in August:* Carnac, Grande Fête des Menhirs. *End of August:* Dinard, Fête de la Jeunesse et de la Mer.

October: Redon, La Bogue d'Or (Golden Husk); Dinan, Fête des Remparts.

See **Folk Festivals**.

Ferries:

P & O Ferries: Portsmouth–Cherbourg; Portsmouth–Le Havre.
Brittany Ferries: Portsmouth–St. Malo; Cork–Roscoff; Plymouth–Roscoff; Portsmouth–Caen.
Sealink: Portsmouth–Cherbourg; Weymouth–Cherbourg.

Fish Auctions: *Les criées* are the early-morning fish auctions in which restaurateurs and housewives compete for lobster, tunny, oysters, crab, sole, *lotte* (monkfish), mullet, fresh sardines and a score of other varieties of fish and crustaceans. The largest are held at Audierne, Concarneau (0700-1000), Douarnenez, Le Guilvinec, Lesconil, Loctudy and St. Guenolé. In Le Croisic, the fish market has lobsters for sale from 0430 and fish from 0600 Mon.-Fri.

Folk Festivals: The Ar Falz movement was started in the 1930s to encourage Breton culture, particularly maintenance of the language (see **A-Z**), traditional dance groups and Breton music. Many old local fêtes have now been revived.
May: St. Brieuc, Le Mai Breton.
Late June/early July: Rennes, Tombées de la Nuit (traditional Breton arts festival).
July: St. Malo, Fête Folklorique du Clos Poulet. *Last week of July:* Quimper, Festival de Cornouaille.
Early August: Lorient, Festival Interceltique (Celtic art and traditions).
Mid August: Guingamp, St. Loup festival of Breton dance; St. Brieuc, Seagull folk festival. *3rd Sun. in August:* Concarneau, Fête des Filets Bleus (folk festival).
See **Events**.

Food: Although Breton cuisine is not in the same class as that of Burgundy or Provence, the traveller will undoubtedly be pleasantly surprised. Certainly one notices immediately the creperies to be found in every town and village. You can make a delicious meal of two or three crepes as different courses. These wafer-thin waffle-pancake sandwiches range in price from 8F to 30F depending on the filling. The simplest of

all are made with sugar and butter. The fillings include chocolate, honey, banana, chestnuts, almonds, caramel, coconut, lemon and three or more different types of *confiture* (jam). *Galettes* contain savoury fillings such as cheese, ham, eggs, sausage, tomato and onion rissoles. *Boulangeries* or patisseries sell crepes in packets for reheating in butter or oil.

The seafood and shellfish dishes are probably the best in France. Lobster, clams, scallops, shrimps and oysters are served fresh, or in a pastry, or stuffed with garlic and herbs. They can be fried in crisp batter, grilled with *coulis* (purée) or try the rich sauce *à l'Armoricaine* as a mousse. Fish dishes include turbot, bass, monkfish (*lotte*) and sole, and fresh river carp, pike, shad, eel and salmon. The fish stew, *cotriade*, is a delicious mix of mackerel, whiting and eel, with scallops, mussels, some vegetables and perhaps Muscadet white wine, mildly flavoured with herbs.

Meat dishes are likely to be local lamb, *potée bretonne* (hotpot with smoked sausages and pork), shin of beef, the ubiquitous *poulet* (Brittany produces a third of French chickens) and duck.

Vegetables are grown all over Brittany and include onions, cauliflowers, artichokes, carrots, peas, beans and potatoes. A dozen local cheeses are also produced, among which are Montalban, Jonchée (sheep's cheese with bay leaves), St. Paulin, Port-Salut and St. Agathon (Guingamp).

There is no local wine apart from Muscadet and Gros-Plant from the Nantes region, but a wide variety of Breton ciders is available from Beg-Meil and Fouesnant, in *brut* (dry), *doux* (sweet) or *bouché* (sparkling) forms. See **RESTAURANTS** topic page by town, **Eating Out**.

Golf: Brittany has more golf courses than any other region of France – a total of 18. They tend to be crowded in the peak months of July and Aug. but during the rest of the year the clubs have plenty of room for visitors. Out of season, green fees average 110F-180F. Many clubs have practice holes and offer temporary memberships.

Morbihan: Golf de St. Laurent, Ploërmel; Golf de Baden, Kernic; Golf de Sauzon, Belle-Île; Golf du Kerver, Le Crouesty.

Finistère: Golf de l'Odet, Clohars-Fouesnant; Golf de Brest-Iroise, Parc

de Lann-Rohou, near Landerneau; Golf de Cornouaille, Manoir de
Meneur, near Concarneau; Golf de Crozon, Crozon; St. Samson, near
Trégastel; Les Ajoncs d'Or, Kergrain-Lantic; Club de Boisgelen, Pléhédel.
Ille et Vilaine-Côte d'Émeraude: Rennes-St.-Jacques-de-la-Lande; St.
Malo-Le Tronchet, near Dinan; Pen Guen, near St. Cast-le-Guildo; Golf
du Château des Ormes, Chaine des Rois, Dol-de-Bretagne; Sables d'Or-
les Pins, Cap Fréhel; Dinard-Golf; Golf de la Freslonnière, Le Rheu, near
Rennes.
See **Sports**.

Health: Medical treatment is available to all citizens of EC countries
through the French social security system. Residents of the UK should
obtain form E111 from the DSS before departure. You will have to pay
for any treatment you receive, then claim it back on your return. Even an
ordinary visit to the doctor costs c. 100F, so it certainly pays to take out
medical insurance beforehand. Lists of doctors, including those who are
available on Sun. and holidays, can be obtained from police stations,
chemists and probably from your hotel. See **Chemists**, **Emergency
Numbers**.

Horse-drawn Carriages: *La roulotte à cheval* is an admirable way
of seeing the Breton countryside. Each caravan is equipped for four persons, with cooking facilities and a detailed guidebook on 'equine maintenance'. Consult the local tourist office for details.

Insurance: You should take out comprehensive travel insurance cov-
ering you and your family against theft and loss of property, car and
money, as well as medical expenses, for the duration of your stay. Your
travel agent, the AA or RAC will be able to recommend a suitable policy.
See **Crime & Theft**, **Driving**, **Health**.

Language: In practical terms you will not need to know any Breton
phrases but it may help to have a basic vocabulary:
Aber = estuary; *Breizh* = Brittany; *Enez* = isle; *Fest-noz* = folk celebra-
tions/party; *Goat/Coat* = wood; *Guic/Gui* = town; *Ker* = village, house;
Lann = church; *Loc* = holy place, monastery; *Men* = stone; *Mor* = sea;

Pen = headland, cape; *Ploe/Plou/Plo* = parish, village; *Traon/Trou* = valley; *Tre/Tref* = place of; *Tre/Trez* = village, hamlet; *Troménies* = pardons.

Laundries: Hotels usually offer a laundry service. Main towns in Brittany now have self-service, coin-operated Launderettes (*laundromat, laverie automatique*), usually open 0800-1900.

Lighthouses: Many lighthouses (*phares*) are open to the public and make an interesting excursion, especially for children. Ask the local tourist office about opening times.
Main lighthouses:
Cap Fréhel, northwest of St. Cast-le-Guildo; Roscoff; Phare de Trézien, Plouarzel, west of Brest; Kermorvan, Le Conquet, west of Brest; Phare du Portzic, southwest of Brest; Plougonvelin, St. Mathieu, west of Brest; Pit Minou Plouzané, west of Brest; Eckmühl, Penmarc'h, southwest of Quimper; Pyramide, 2 rue du Phare, Bénodet.

Lost Property: If you lose anything you should contact the Bureau des Objets Trouvés in large towns. In smaller towns ask the hotel or camp site manager for advice or visit the police station.

Markets: Markets open early and close at midday when you may get some bargains. However, most towns also have a large covered market open 0700-1800. Also look out for *marchés d'artisans* (local crafts) or ask the tourist office for details. See the appropriate town entry in the cultural/historical gazetteer for its main market days. See **Artisans**, **Best Buys**, **Fish Auctions**, **Shopping**.

Auray

Money: Every town in Brittany has a wide choice of banks which open 0900-1630 Mon.-Fri. There are exchange facilities at airports and main-line railway stations (Rennes, Brest, Quimper), as well as in most tourist offices (useful at weekends). Most main post offices have currency-exchange facilities, often with a low rate of commission. Cities have a number of bureaux de change in the centre and near the railway station. Exchange rates and commissions vary, so it pays to look around. Credit cards are widely accepted with Visa (Carte Bleue) being the most common. Traveller's cheques are probably the safest way to carry your money on holiday and can be used in many locations, though not in the smaller hotels and restaurants. They are easy to change at any bank or bureau de change but don't forget to take your passport. See **Currency**.

Music: There is no indigenous music other than folklore songs in Brittany but the main towns have regular concert seasons of classical, jazz and pop music. Ask the tourist office for a programme of events. See **Events**, **Folk Festivals**, **What's On**.

Newspapers: A wide range of newspapers can be bought at pavement newsstands. English-language papers are rare but are available at three times the UK price in high season. See **What's On**.

Nightlife: Generally speaking, holiday-makers in Brittany are not likely to find a great deal of nightlife. However, the resort casinos offer quite sophisticated entertainment. In addition, there are discos and clubs but these are often closed out of season. Expect to pay an entrance fee of 50F-60F per head. There are many cinemas showing French or American films but these are rarely dubbed in English. The larger cities have a Maison de la Culture which offers a year-long programme of entertainment, including theatre, jazz, pop concerts, etc. There is the occasional bistro-cabaret such as Chez Paul in Quimper; Le Sinclair, Rue Kéreon in Brest; and New Club and Rétro-Sillon, Chaussée de Sion in St. Malo. The tourist office should be able to give you up-to-date details; ask for the leaflet called *Spectacles, Informations*.

Opening Times:
Banks – 0900-1200, 1400-1630 Mon.-Fri. (busy central branches stay open at lunchtime).
Bureaux de change – 0830/0900/0930-1800/2200 Mon.-Sat.
Offices – 0830-1200, 1400-1800 Mon.-Sat.
Post offices – 0800-1900 Mon.-Fri., 0800-1200 Sat.
Restaurants – Usually 1200-1400, 1900-2200. Many close on Mon., a few close for Aug. and many close for the winter months.
Shops – Vary enormously between 0800 and 1900 but smaller shops close 1200-1400, while others may close on Mon.
Museums, chateaux and monuments – Usually 1000-1800 July and Aug. Smaller sites close for lunch. All have reduced hours out of season. Many are closed on Tue.

Orientation: Most town tourist offices supply a basic street map free of charge. If you are lost ask, 'Où est la route pour X?'

Parking: Parking in the centre of Rennes, Brest, St. Malo, Vannes and Quimper is always difficult but less so in St. Brieuc and the inland towns. Parking meters operate 0900-1200 and 1400-1900 but police or traffic wardens can impose fines or tow away vehicles parked illegally. If your vehicle is impounded, telephone the town hall (*mairie*) to reclaim it. Parking is often free on Sun. See **Driving**.

Passports & Customs: A passport from Britain, Ireland or the EC allows a 90-day stay with no visa required. Also acceptable are British visitors' passports and excursion passes (available from post offices). If you wish to stay for more than 90 days, contact the local French police station or the Service des Étrangers in Rennes at 21 rue Général Maurice Guillaudot, tel: 99387811. Citizens from other countries, including the USA, Canada, Australia and New Zealand, require a visa which is easily obtained from French embassies and consulates in those countries.

Petrol: Petrol (*l'essence*) is available by the litre, and prices are clearly marked in petrol stations (0800-2100), which are usually self-service.

There are two grades: *super* and *essence*. Leaded petrol is *plomb*. Supermarkets always discount their petrol prices. See **Driving**.

Police: The town police, *police municipale*, wear dark blue uniforms and flat caps. Outside the towns they wear white belts, black jackets and blue trousers. Always address them as 'Monsieur (or Madame) l'Agent'; they are usually helpful to tourists. Any theft should be reported to the nearest police station (*commissariat de police*). To back up a possible insurance claim you can obtain a free certificate confirming you have reported a *perte* (loss) or *vol* (theft).
Main police stations:
Brest: 2 rue Rameau; Dinan: Rue de la Garaye; Dinard: Pl. de la Gare; Quimper: Rue Théodore le Hars; Rennes: 21 rue Général Maurice Guillaudot and Bd. de la Tour d'Auvergne; St. Brieuc: Rue Jouallan; St. Malo: Pl. des Frères Lamennais; Vannes: 13 bd. de la Paix.
See **Crime & Theft**, **Emergency Numbers**.

Post Offices: Look for their yellow signs marked PTT or Postes (postboxes are the same colour). They provide full postal services, as well as telephones for both local and long-distance calls. Telephones can be metered and calls paid for afterwards. Often a currency exchange service is available. Postage stamps can also be purchased from *tabacs*.
Main post offices:
Brest: Pl. Général Leclerc; Dinan: Pl. Duclos; Dinard: Pl. de la République; Quimper: Bd. Amiral de Kerguelen; Rennes: Rue Alma and Pl. de la République (Palais de Commerce); St. Brieuc: 11 rue Michelet; St. Malo: 1 bd. de la Tour d'Auvergne; Vannes: Pl. de la République.
See **Opening Times**.

Public Holidays: 1 Jan., Easter Mon., 1 May, 8 May, Ascension Day (40 days after Easter), Whit Mon., 14 July, 15 Aug., 11 Nov. and 25 Dec. Banks close at noon on the nearest working day before a public holiday.

Rabies: Still exists here as in other parts of France. All animal bites should be treated immediately by a doctor.

Railways: SNCF. The high-speed train (TGV) now leaves Paris-Montparnasse for Brest via Le Mans, Vitré, Rennes (2 hr), St. Brieuc and Morlaix. French railways are renowned for their fast, comfortable, punctual and clean trains.

Always remember to validate your ticket in a small orange machine (*composteur*) which clips and dates your ticket before you enter the platform; otherwise you could be fined on the train. A variety of cheaper tickets is available and it is advisable to purchase these before your journey from the French Railways office in Piccadilly, London, next to the French Government Tourist Office.

Main railway stations:

Brest: Pl. 19ème RIC; Dinan: Pl. du 11 Novembre; Dinard: Rue de la Gare; Quimper: Av. de la Libération; Rennes: Pl. de la Gare; St. Brieuc: 5 bd. Charner; St. Malo: Pl. Jean Coquelin; Vannes: Av. Farre et Lincy.

Religious Services: France is predominantly a Roman Catholic country, but churches of most denominations can be found in Brittany. Consult tourist offices for times of services.

Shopping: All Breton towns have a full range of modern shopping facilities from giant *hypermarchés* to specialist shops such as *charcuteries* (pork butchers), patisseries, *chocolateries* and *boulangeries*. Most towns have a fruit and vegetable market (see **A-Z**) and the fishing ports their early-morning fish auctions (see **A-Z**). All prices are fixed and no bargaining is required. See **Best Buys**, **Opening Times**.

Smoking: Smoking is not permitted in churches, museums, art galleries and theatres, and is discouraged in restaurants. Trains have separate non-smoking compartments.

Son et Lumière: These are usually historical pageants involving a large cast, and are performed throughout the summer in an open-air setting, usually using a chateau as a backdrop. Expect to pay 80F-100F (less for children) for an entertaining evening. Shows take place at Châteaugiron, Dinard, Vitré, Suscinio, Vannes and Forteresse de Largoët. Ask at tourist offices for details.

Sports: Horse riding, walking on the Grandes Randonnées, rock-climbing (St. Just, Bains-sur-Oust, Mézières-sur-Couesnon), hang-gliding, archery, canal- and river-fishing for salmon, trout, eel and shad, boating and canoeing are some of the activities the region has to offer. There are also flying schools at Dinard, Redon, Rennes and St. Malo, and a municipal *piscine* for swimming and hard tennis courts in every large village. A useful contact for walkers, horse riders and cyclists is the Association Bretonne des Relais et Itinéraires, 3 rue des Portes Mordelaises, 3500 Rennes, tel: 99315944. See **Golf, Water Sports**.

Taxis: All towns in Brittany have taxis readily available. They can also be found at airports, railway stations and taxi ranks, or ordered by telephone. Taxis are metered but if your journey is out of town check beforehand whether you have to pay for the driver's return journey.

Telephones & Telegrams: You will find numerous payphones but the majority require a phonecard. Coin-operated machines take 1F, 5F and 10F coins. Phonecards (*télécartes*) are available from post offices and *tabacs* and cost 50F and 100F. To use a cardphone, lift the receiver, insert the card, pull down the handle above it and dial. In post offices you can use a metered telephone which lets you make the call before paying. If using a café telephone you may have to buy a *jeton* (token) at the bar. Calls from your hotel room will be charged at a premium.

Cheap rates are 2130-0800 Mon.-Fri., after 1400 Sat. and all day Sun. and holidays. To telephone the UK from France, dial 19, wait for the tone to change, dial 44 (11 for the USA, 61 for Australia), then the STD number minus the first 0, then the number. You can receive return calls at telephone booths. All post offices accept domestic and overseas telegrams. You can dictate a telegram by dialling 3655.

Television & Radio: There are six channels on French TV: TF1, A2, FR3, LA5, M6 and Canal + (the first paying and coded network). News broadcasts are at 0800, 1300, 2000 and 2300. French radio broadcasts in French on FM but it is possible to receive BBC Radio 4 by tuning in to 1500 m on long wave, and 463 m medium wave for the BBC World Service.

Tides: Beach resorts, hotels and camp sites have tide timetables so that activities can be planned. On some parts of the coast several kilometres of shore are exposed at low tide. Only bathe with confidence on main beaches manned by lifeguards. Green and red flags are flown for safety and danger.

Time Difference: French standard time is GMT plus 1 hr and the clocks go forward 1 hr in summer, making France 1 hr ahead of Britain, although there are a few weeks in autumn when the times are the same.

Tipping: A 15% service charge is included in your bill at all hotels and restaurants, as is TVA (VAT), so there is no need to leave a tip unless you feel the service has been particularly good. If you pay by cash, any small change is usually left for the waiter. Hotel porters expect to receive 10F per item of luggage, chambermaids 10F per day, taxi drivers 10-15% of the fare and hairdressers about 10F.

Toilets: Usually to be found in railway stations, main squares and more frequently as modern unisex metallic cabins which need a 2F coin. The muzak is free! Out-of-town petrol stations offer free facilities, and in restaurant, hotel and museum toilets you may meet an attendant who requires a small tip.

Trégastel

Tourist Information: Brittany takes tourism very seriously.
Consequently, there are many *offices de tourisme* or *syndicats d'initiative*. They are usually helpful, have a wide range of leaflets and
maps, and will probably make hotel reservations for you (some make a
charge for this service). However, the staff rarely speak English. Offices
usually open 0900-1800 Mon.-Fri., 0900-1200, 1400-1800 Sat. but
are closed Sun. except during festivals.
Main tourist offices:
Brest: 1 pl. de la Liberté, tel: 98442496; Dinan: 6 rue de l'Horloge,
tel: 96397540; Dinard: 2 bd. Féart, tel: 99469412; Quimper: 3 rue Roi
Gradlon, tel: 98950469; Rennes: Pont de Nemours, tel: 99790198;
St. Brieuc: 7 rue St. Guèno, tel: 96333250; St. Malo: Esplanade St.
Vincent, tel: 99566448; Vannes: 1 rue Thiers, tel: 97472434.
See **Accommodation**, **What's On**.

Transport: See **Airports**, **Buses**, **Ferries**, **Railways**, **Taxis**.

Traveller's Cheques: See **Money.**

Walks: The Grandes Randonnées trails with their noticeable red and white waymarks criss-cross Brittany. The ABRI office at 9 rue des Portes Mordelaises, Rennes, tel: 99315944, will give you advice, sell you *Topoguides* and inform you of the whereabouts of a hundred or so *gîtes d'étape* (walkers' bed and breakfast establishments). There are also 1500 km of walks along the 37 canal and river towpaths throughout the region. Known as the Tour de Bretagne, the GR 34 runs along the whole north coast for a total of 840 km. The GR 37 starts southeast of Brest and meanders eastwards to Josselin, Becherel and Vitré. The GR 41 runs for 90 km from St. Brieuc to Lannion and the GR 38 runs from Douarnenez to Rochefort-en-Terre and Redon.

Water Sports: Along Brittany's immense coastline, every form of nautical activity is available. Water-skiing, windsurfing, underwater diving, deep-sea angling, swimming from scores of golden beaches and regattas galore make it the most popular 'marine' region in France. Called *ports de plaisance*, there are no fewer than 60 marinas scattered along the coast. Three key 'sailing towns' are Pleneuf, Perros-Guirec and Crozon-Morgat. The Round France races (July) start at Perros-Guirec, Brest is the start of the 24 hr windsurfing race in mid-Mar., the autumn Rum Route race starts from St. Malo and transatlantic races begin at Lorient. There are regattas in most of the large resorts during the season. There are also about 70 sailing schools, usually at the marinas. A useful address is the Comité de Liaison des Activités Nautiques, 5 rue René-Malec, 2900 Quimper, tel: 98957116. See **Sports**.

What's On: Tourist offices in the larger towns offer a free French-language listings newssheet giving details of local events. Examples are *Dinard Magazine* and *Brest Pratique*. See **Events**, **Newspapers**.

Youth Hostels: The Association Bretonne des Auberges de Jeunesse, La Haute-Boë, 35133 Fleur Igné, tel: 99952873, will supply details.

This book was produced using QuarkXPress™ and Adobe
Illustrator™ on Apple Macintosh™ computers and output to
separated film on a Scantext™ 2030 PD Imagesetter

Text: Patrick Delaforce
Photography: Stuart Boreham
Electronic Cartography: Morton Ward Associates

First published 1993
Copyright © HarperCollins Publishers
Published by HarperCollins Publishers
Printed in Hong Kong
ISBN 0 00 435912-7